The *Accidental Feminist*

How Elizabeth Taylor Raised Our Consciousness and We Were Too Distracted by Her Beauty to Notice

M. G. Lord

Walker & Company
New York

Published by Walker Publishing Company, Inc., New York
A Division of Bloomsbury Publishing

All papers used by Walker & Company are natural, recyclable products made from wood grown in well-managed forests. The manufacturing processes conform to the environmental regulations of the country of origin.

LIBRARY OF CONGRESS CATALOGING-IN-PUBLICATION DATA

Lord, M. G.
The accidental feminist : how Elizabeth Taylor raised our consciousness and we were too distracted by her beauty to notice / M. G. Lord.
p. cm.
Includes bibliographical references and index.
ISBN 978-0-8027-1669-9
1. Taylor, Elizabeth, 1932–2011. 2. Motion picture actors and actresses—United States—Biography. I. Title.
PN2287.T18L67 2012
791.4302'8092—dc23
[B]
2011038047

Visit Walker & Company's Web site at www.walkerbooks.com

1 3 5 7 9 10 8 6 4 2

Typeset by Westchester Book Group
Printed in the U.S.A. by Quad/Graphics, Fairfield, Pennsylvania

For Shannon Halwes,
without whom this book would not exist

Contents

The *Accidental Feminist*

I

The Beautiful Somnambulist

YOU COULD SAY it began in 1944 with *National Velvet*, when Elizabeth Taylor, age twelve, dressed as a boy and stole America's collective heart. By "it," I mean the subversive drumbeats of feminism, which swelled in the star's important movies over decades from a delicate pitty-pat to a resounding roar.

Feminism may not be the first thing that comes to mind when you hear the name Elizabeth Taylor. But it might if you share your definition with writer Rebecca West: "I myself have never been able to find out precisely what feminism is. I only know that people call me a feminist when I express sentiments that differentiate me from a doormat."

Elizabeth Taylor has been called many things, but never doormat—not in life and not on screen. (Except in *Ash Wednesday*, her 1973 movie, where that was the point.) The characters she played were women to be reckoned with. And many of her roles—the great and the not-so-great—surreptitiously brought feminist issues to American audiences held captive by those violet eyes and that epic beauty. While I know that writers and directors create movies, stars create a brand. And the Taylor brand deserves credit for its under-the-radar challenge to traditional attitudes: a woman may not control her sexuality; she may not have an abortion; she may not play with the boys; she may not choose to live without a man; she must obey her husband; and should she speak of unpleasantness, she will be silenced.

Although I love quoting West's glib retort, feminism is, in fact, a tricky thing to define, because its self-identified adherents don't always march in ideological lockstep. To theorist bell hooks, it is "a movement to end sexism, sexist exploitation, and oppression." To writer Marie Shear, it is "the radical notion that women are people." To columnist Katha Pollitt, it is "a social justice movement dedicated to the social, political, economic, and cultural equality of women and men, and to the right of every woman to set her own course." To author Rebecca Walker, it is "to integrate an ideology of equality and female empowerment into the very fiber of my life."

Throughout its history, feminism has never been either monolithic or static. During the twentieth century, its concerns changed from suffrage, temperance, and the repeal of primogeniture laws to reproductive rights, workplace equality, and protection from discrimination based on gender or sexual orientation. Betty Friedan kicked off the so-called second wave of feminism with her 1963 book, *The Feminine Mystique.* In 1971, Gloria Steinem, another second-wave figure, launched *Ms.* magazine to address ongoing feminist issues. But during the magazine's first decade, its readership, like feminism itself, was largely white, heterosexual, and middle class.

In the 1980s, novelist Alice Walker, a *Ms.* contributor, broke with this movement, urging feminists of color to identify as "womanist." A decade later, her daughter Rebecca Walker rejected the "womanist" idea, declaring herself and those who share her views to be "the third wave." Third-wave feminists pitch a big tent—large enough to contain diverse ethnicities, sexual preferences, and gender identities. They affirm their right to sexual pleasure, believing that desire is complex, and consensual behavior should not be policed. All feminists support equal pay for equal work. But despite the consensus, this goal seems no closer to realization than it was fifty years ago. My understanding of feminism derives mostly from second-wave texts. But I admire efforts to make feminism more inclusive, and view controversy within its ranks as a sign of its vitality.

Until a few years ago, I thought the last word on Taylor was written by Camille Paglia in the 1990s. In an important essay, "Elizabeth Taylor: Hollywood's Pagan Queen," Paglia identified in Taylor the ancient, "mythic" sexual power associated with Delilah, Salome, and Helen of Troy. But after watching Taylor's key movies recently with some much younger friends, I discovered what had been hidden in plain sight: the feminist content in some of her iconic films. Be it accidental or deliberate—text or subtext—this content is very much there.

I am a baby boomer. The friends who opened my eyes are Gen X and Gen Y; our age difference changed how we saw things. On a recent Memorial Day weekend, we rented a house together in Palm Springs—that museum of midcentury Hollywood, where the very streets are named for its famous former residents: Frank Sinatra, Bob Hope, and Dinah Shore.

I am old enough to remember these performers in their heyday. My friends are not. They know them, of course, but in their later-life incarnations: Frank Sinatra as a pal of First Lady Nancy Reagan, Bob Hope as a has-been comic, and Dinah Shore as a talk show host. The Gen X friends mostly knew Taylor as the butt of Joan Rivers's fat jokes from the 1980s: Taylor was the woman with "more chins than a Chinese phone book." My Gen Y friends knew her only as a gay icon and an AIDS philanthropist. So when I proposed watching some Taylor DVDs that I had received as a present, my friends expected an evening of camp. Instead, we were gobsmacked—both by Taylor's performances and by her movies' feminist messages.

National Velvet is a sly critique of gender discrimination in sports. Taylor's character, Velvet Brown, falls in love with her horse—a time-honored preteen tradition. She dreams of riding the horse to victory in the Grand National, the most important steeplechase in the world. But because jockeys are required to be male, Velvet is excluded. First crushed, then emboldened, she enters the race anyway, impersonating a boy.

Following *National Velvet*, Taylor's next significant hit was *A Place in the Sun* (1951), which is hard to view as anything other than an abortion-rights movie. It deals with the tragic consequences of stigmatizing unwed pregnancy. Feminism holds that women have a right to control the reproductive use of their bodies. Condemning single mothers relinquishes that power to men. "Mothers were said not to give life to new individuals, so much as to give children to their husbands, so that male surnames and inheritances might be perpetuated," explains author Barbara Walker in *The Skeptical Feminist.*

Feminism also endorses a woman's right to control her sexuality. In *BUtterfield 8* (1960), Taylor's character is censured not for being a prostitute but for exercising her right to choose the men with whom she will sleep. This galls the men who desire her, especially the ones she rejects. Other movies explore different feminist themes: *Giant* (1956) deals with the feminization of the American West; *Suddenly, Last Summer* (1959) portrays the callousness of the male medical establishment toward women patients; *The Sandpiper* (1965) pits goddess-centered paganism against patriarchal monotheism. Taylor's most celebrated movie, *Who's Afraid of Virginia Woolf?* (1966), may also be her most feminist. It demonstrates what happens to a woman when the only way that society permits her to express herself is through her husband's career and children.

Before going into the world to preach, zealots of all stripes retreat to the desert to meditate and prepare. After my exile in Palm Springs (getting massages and lounging by the pool), I returned to Los Angeles with a mission: learn more about these films and the circumstances under which they were made. And if their feminist content held up, spread the word.

★ ★ ★

A few years earlier, when I met Taylor, no link between her and feminism had yet crossed my mind. I did, however, see a vast disconnect between her shallow tabloid persona and the seeming depths of her real-life self. Intelligence flickered behind those lilac eyes. In October 2001, Taylor spoke at a small dedication ceremony for the Roddy McDowall Memorial Rose Garden at the Motion Picture and Television Fund's Wasserman Campus, which was then a retirement home for show people. Adam Kurtzman, an artist who sculpted a bronze portrait of McDowall for the garden, invited me to the ceremony, which I could not otherwise have attended. Taylor stood next to Sybil Burton Christopher, Richard Burton's first wife, and, to my surprise, embraced her. The tabloids had written at length about the two women's enmity, which began when Richard left Sybil for Elizabeth. But their reconciliation was apparently not salacious enough to report. At the end of his life, McDowall had brought them together. Elizabeth held one of his hands, Sybil, the other, easing his passage from this world to the next.

In my notebook, about Taylor's appearance, I wrote, "Not bald." In 1997, Taylor had allowed *Life* magazine to photograph her with a shaved head, before surgery for a benign brain tumor. The *National Enquirer*, of course, published all manner of macabre unauthorized shots. Taylor was gold to the gutter press; so much so that after her death on March 23, 2011, the *New York Times* ran a tribute from a tabloid reporter describing his botched attempt to balloon over her 1991 wedding to construction worker Larry Fortensky.

Artists, I realize, are rarely as interesting as their art. Yet as writer Walker Percy observed in his 1961 novel, *The Moviegoer*, stars of Taylor's magnitude possess "an aura of heightened reality" that moves with them, and "all who fall within it feel it."

The aura has a dark side. We view film stars with "a kind of possessiveness, in which they both submit to and evade our goggle-eyed wonder," critic Leo Braudy said in *The Frenzy of Renown: Fame and Its History*. Most stars harden in response to this attention. They have to. They must withstand the projections of a million strangers.

Nor do such stars inhabit anything resembling the real world. I grasped this when I interviewed the actor Kevin McCarthy, who was still matinee-idol handsome at age ninety-four in 2008. (McCarthy died in 2010.) He had known Taylor through his close friend, Montgomery Clift. In 2002, McCarthy and his wife, Kate, were guests of Liza Minnelli at her wedding to David Gest. Taylor and actress Marisa Berenson served as matrons of honor. But the ceremony had to be delayed for an hour. Because Taylor had *forgotten her shoes.*

Taylor has had many biographers. Yet their books often reveal more about their authors than about her. Some dish; some fawn; few paint a nuanced picture. To the scandalmongers, for instance, Elizabeth's mother, Sara Taylor, was a failed actress who morphed into a monomaniacal stage mother. But Kate Burton, Richard's daughter, a Broadway actress who remained close to her former stepmother, tells a different story: "Elizabeth was very devoted to her mother, who lived to be very elderly. And she was *absolutely* devoted to her father."

Other biographers fixate on Taylor's anatomy, as if that alone explained her. Ellis Amburn, for example, treats her breasts as if they were independent entities—like children or pets. After charting their arrival during her teens, he tells how Metro-Goldwyn-Mayer, the studio where Taylor was under contract, dealt with them: hiring "Bust Inspectors" to patrol the sets. To determine whether a neckline was too revealing, an inspector placed an orange in the space between her breasts: "If the cameraman could see the orange, he had to move the camera back."

Not all of Taylor's biographers have admired her. Brenda Maddox, an American-born, Harvard-educated writer who now lives in England, took on Taylor in 1977. Maddox is known for two probing, judicious books: *Nora: The Real Life of Molly Bloom*, about James Joyce's wife, and *Rosalind Franklin: The Dark Lady of DNA*, about the scientist whose premature death from ovarian cancer allowed biologists Francis Crick and James Watson to claim credit for her work. But Maddox's take on Taylor is, well, unhinged. Her collection of damning details—to the exclusion of anything positive—makes the 1981 biography of Taylor by renowned hatchet-wielder Kitty Kelley look like a mash note. In fairness, Maddox doesn't just hate Taylor, she hates every artifact of American popular culture that doesn't "indict" some aspect of American life.

When a biographer attacks a subject who is in midlife, the biographer risks generating a flawed book. The subject's identity can change dramatically in the final four or five decades of life, as it did with Elizabeth Taylor. In 1985, she began fundraising for AIDS—when so much fear and mystery surrounded the disease that doors were slammed in her face. "Elizabeth did something when it required real courage," Elton John told an interviewer in 2007. "She didn't just put her name to a cause or speak from an ivory tower: She lobbied, she got out on the streets, she formed her own foundation."

Similarly, early in her career, Taylor may not have noticed the feminist content that undergirded some of her roles. Like the beautiful somnambulist in Harold Lloyd's *High and Dizzy*, who sleepwalked onto an upper-story ledge, Taylor strode unconsciously into risky territory, unaware of just how "out-there" she was. Somewhere along the line, though, I think Taylor woke up.

Taylor's 1987 diet book, *Elizabeth Takes Off*, repeatedly makes feminist points—exploring ideas about women and body image that English therapist Susie Orbach first brought to widespread attention in her groundbreaking 1978 book, *Fat Is a Feminist Issue*. Taylor professes her admiration for Gloria Steinem, particularly the way Steinem handled an oft-heard comment on aging: You don't look forty. "This is what forty looks like," she recalls Steinem saying.

No examination of Taylor would be complete without the Hollywood institutions that she grew up under, clashed with, and ultimately helped to defeat. One was the Production Code Administration, a group of ruthless and astonishingly powerful men who between 1934 and 1966 routinely bowdlerized scripts and excised logic from plots to prevent films from criticizing religious authority or the institution of marriage. Another was the so-called studio system, which locked actors into long-term contracts, requiring them to work for flat fees, and denying them a choice in their roles.

In exchange for job security, actors signed away every aspect of their lives. Studio publicists invented fictions to conceal behavior that might hurt a star at the box office: drinking, drugging, philandering, or any activity modified by the adjective "homosexual." Sham marriages were commonplace. In 1955, actor Rock Hudson wedded his agent's secretary to banish rumors of his gayness. Some stars delivered their best performances in their counterfeit lives. In *Kate*, his provocative biography of Katharine Hepburn, writer William Mann offers convincing evidence that the legendary extramarital affair between Hepburn and Spencer Tracy was, in fact, a cover-up for both stars, who, in their truly private "private lives," were gay.

As a young woman Taylor, too, played the duplicity game. But in 1962, after two men in sequence very publicly ditched their wives for her, she stopped hiding. And far from suffering at the box office, she became Hollywood's highest-paid actress. Not even the Vatican could hold her back. When its weekly newspaper, *L'Osservatore della Domenica*, accused her of "erotic vagrancy," she blithely quipped, "Can I sue the Pope?"

In mining Taylor's films for their feminist content, I could start out on a safe path with *Who's Afraid of Virginia Woolf?*, a blue-chip movie securely ensconced on many respected critics' top-ten lists. What I discovered, though, was that some of Taylor's so-called turkeys were anything but. This is especially true after 1961, when she chose her own projects, rather than having them imposed by MGM. These later films often had ahead-of-the-curve messages that made people squirm. It was easier to sneer at a film than to come to grips with its prescient subtext. Or as Clement Greenberg famously observed, "All profoundly original art looks ugly at first."

I hope this book will move readers to watch the movies it highlights with an open mind, to see if they, too, perceive the feminist content. I especially hope the Millennial Generation will watch, catching a glimpse of a recent past in which rights they take for granted—abortion, interracial marriage, and certain sexual acts in private between consenting adults—were illegal.

Inspired by the retrograde gender roles in such popular TV shows as *Mad Men*, some males born long after the bad-boy days have begun to express nostalgia for them. Just once, they'd like to harass a female co-worker with impunity, or force a gay man who criticizes their clothing back into his soundproof closet. The rights hard-won by second-wave feminists might still be taken away. Abortion, for instance, remains a hot-button issue, and given the allegiance of some Supreme Court justices to patriarchal cults, *Roe v. Wade* may not be the final word.

Taylor's films show the bad-boy days as they really

were—which was not so great if you happened to be female. Or as Laura Reynolds, Taylor's character in *The Sandpiper*, laments: "The man is a husband and a father *and* something else, say a doctor. The woman is a wife and mother *and* . . . nothing. And it's the nothing that kills her."

2

National Velvet, 1944

Velvet Brown! Who do you think you are? —Mickey Rooney as Mi Taylor, a horse trainer in *National Velvet*

Why, I am the owner of the Pie. —Elizabeth Taylor, confidently, as Velvet Brown

And does that give you leave to go poking your head out amongst the stars? Mi continues, *believing you could take the richest grandest prize a horse ever won? . . . You're just a wisp of butcher's daughter in a cold stable late at night when you'd better to be in bed with a doll.*

TO APPRECIATE THE SLY SEDITION in Enid Bagnold's novel, *National Velvet*, one must know how women were treated in the time and place where it is set: England between the two world wars. To glean such knowledge swiftly—as one might from CliffsNotes—one can read Virginia Woolf's *Three Guineas*, a blistering, book-length essay published in 1938,

In the essay, Woolf—best known for her modernist novels, *Mrs. Dalloway* and *To the Lighthouse*—rages against nearly every British institution that ever demeaned the intelligence or belittled the aspirations or crushed the soul of a woman. There were many—from the primogeniture laws (which precluded daughters from inheriting property) to the voting laws (which until 1928 kept women away from the polls) to the convention of educating sons instead of daughters (which prevented Woolf herself from obtaining a university education).

Sons needed formal schooling, the reasoning went, because they were expected to support their future wives and children. But what if wives themselves could earn a living? Woolf mocks the notion that wives and husbands share equally in a husband's income—unless, of course, a wife is insanely altruistic. Otherwise, why would she devote thousands of pounds to "clubs to which her own sex is not admitted" or to "colleges from which her own sex is excluded" or—as Bagnold herself might have wondered—to "racecourses where she may not ride"?

This brings us to *National Velvet*—in which a girl jockey leaps over the racecourse gender barrier. Don't be deceived by the book's sweet colloquial language or its folksy village setting. It is as fierce a polemic as *Three Guineas*.

The actress Elizabeth Taylor was also a product of England in the 1930s. She was born in London on February 27, 1932. Her parents, Francis and Sara Taylor, were American. But until she moved with them and her older brother Howard to Los Angeles in 1939, Taylor's world was Bagnold's world was Woolf's world.

National Velvet was published in 1935 and sold well enough for Metro-Goldwyn-Mayer to option it—not necessarily to make a movie from it but to keep the property away from competing studios. Young Elizabeth read the book and loved it, or so she blurted to Clarence Brown, an American director who wanted to film it. The blurt appeared spontaneous—a bubbly remark made during a chance meeting with the director. But it was, in fact, calculated—part of a campaign that she and her mother mounted to cultivate Brown, which also included sending him handmade birthday cards and Valentines. The exchange occurred inside MGM, where Taylor, age eleven, had newly become a contract player.

After the Taylor family settled in Los Angeles, Taylor's mother, a former actress, took Elizabeth to auditions, and the little girl bagged minor parts in *There's One Born Every Minute* (1942), *Lassie Come Home* (1943), *Jane Eyre* (1944), and *The White Cliffs of Dover* (1944). But Elizabeth wanted more. She wanted to participate in the movie equivalent of the Grand National Sweepstakes. She wanted to portray Velvet Brown.

Elizabeth quickly charmed Pandro S. Berman, producer of *National Velvet.* When she came to his office, he admired her spirit. But he told her that she was too small. No audience would accept her as a world-class rider. So Taylor *willed* herself to grow. Months later, Taylor returned to Berman's office. And in an incident that MGM publicity exploded into legend, Berman measured Taylor's height and gave her the part.

Taylor's biographers don't agree on how many—or even whether—Taylor added inches. Whether Taylor truly grew—or her stage mother and MGM connived to create this impression—seems almost irrelevant. Given a choice between a great story and a true story, the 1940s movie press unhesitatingly went with great.

Fortunately for Taylor, screenwriters Helen Deutsch and Theodore Reeves crafted a script that was even stronger than Bagnold's book. They pared out extraneous characters and confusing scenes. And they freighted the film with metaphor. *National Velvet* didn't just inspire women who yearned to be jockeys. Nor did it merely foreshadow Title IX, the 1972 federal law that created opportunities for women athletes. It spoke to all little girls who refused to let their gender compromise their dreams.

Velvet Brown is a prepubescent avatar of Leslie Lynnton Benedict, Taylor's character in the 1956 movie *Giant.* Even in childhood, Velvet is strong and centered, with a deep connection to nature. She loves horses enough to mold "the Pie," her cherished gelding, into a champion. Velvet lives on the English seacoast—not a balmy surfside playground but a harsh, rocky landscape. A place where toughness and beauty coincide. And where the hills, as Bagnold describes them, tumble down to the ocean, "like the rumps of elephants . . . like a starlit herd of divine pigs."

Clarence Brown, the film's director, couldn't shoot the specific rumps and pigs to which Bagnold had referred. During World War II, the English seacoast was fortified against a Nazi attack. So he built Velvet's village—cobblestone streets and thatched roofs—on a soundstage in Culver City, California. For the film's exterior shots, he went north, to Monterey County, California, where the coastal breeze is as damp as England's and the bluffs plummet to the sea. When Velvet gallops there, even jaded viewers feel some magic. They may not believe—as Velvet does—that she rides "an enchanted horse with invisible wings." But few pick up on the real-life identity of the setting: the ninth and tenth holes of the Pebble Beach Golf Links.

Bagnold's characters speak in koans, most of which the screenwriters preserved. But her plot was a mess—in need of Deutsch and Reeves to streamline it. In the book, for example, Velvet doesn't win one special horse in a raffle, as she does in the movie. Instead, she is inundated with horses. One day, out of the blue, Velvet meets a man she once encountered at an equestrian event. She walks with him through his stable, where he scribbles something on a scrap of paper. He then hands her the scrap, marches off, and shoots himself. In the head. For absolutely no reason. Velvet is of course freaked out. But she perks up quickly. Because the man randomly willed all his horses to her.

In contrast, the movie unfolds in clear scenes that follow a logical course. Hard to believe, but in 1944, Mickey Rooney was a bigger star than Taylor—so the film initially focuses on him. He portrays Mi Taylor—a damaged youth, unemployed and homeless. Although he was once a crackerjack jockey, Mi refuses to ride, because, we learn later, he survived a racing accident that killed his best friend. The accident rattled him, eroding his confidence. Had a different actress been cast as

Velvet, Rooney might have "owned" the picture. But the moment Taylor appears—in a rustic village schoolroom—she magnetizes the camera. And *National Velvet* belongs to her.

Bagnold's Velvet lacked Taylor's beauty. She was anorexic, or, as Bagnold writes, "thin as famine . . . like a child model for a head of Death," which only in recent years has become fashionable in Hollywood. To correct her protruding teeth, she requires a snap-in orthodontic device—which Taylor, in the movie, also occasionally wears. (To make the appliance fit, Taylor's mom forced her daughter to have her healthy baby teeth extracted—a painful ordeal that, in Kitty Kelley's view, proves Sara to be a ruthless stage mother.)

In the film, Velvet bonds quickly with the Pie—abridged from "Piebald" in the book. When the horse bolts from his owner's meadow—and gallops menacingly toward town—Velvet steps forward to obstruct his path. Terrified, Mi is certain Velvet will be killed. But the horse rears back, sees Velvet, and stops. In an instant. Causing the viewer to realize: this is neither an ordinary horse nor an ordinary girl.

Velvet's father, however, is relentlessly ordinary. Not evil, just dull—and filled with his own importance. But by an amazing stroke of luck, he snared an extraordinary wife—a generous, accomplished woman who at age twenty swam the English Channel. In Edwardian England, as Virginia Woolf wrote, women of all classes were permitted to have only one career: marriage. Yet instead of chafing at this limitation, Mrs. Brown surmounts it. She taught herself to manage Mr.

Brown—to implement her wise ideas by convincing him that they are his.

Every time he blusters, she teases him. When the Pie falls ill, Mi and Velvet nurse the horse through the night. But the next day, when he shows improvement, Velvet runs to school—and Mr. Brown chides Mrs. Brown for not forcing her to rest. "I like the spirit that makes her want to go out after staying up all night," Mrs. Brown replies. But when he keeps on criticizing, she stops him: Velvet will "be back in half an hour. This is Saturday and there is no school."

Of course Mr. Brown opposes Velvet's plan to enter the Grand National. It's preposterous—and they can't afford the fee. But in her daughter, Mrs. Brown detects an ancient spark—the same spark that set her aflame when her detractors jeered, or "said a woman couldn't swim the English Channel." She refuses to let her husband snuff that spark out.

The Browns do not share equally in the household wealth. Mr. Brown controls it. But Mrs. Brown will not back down. She brings Velvet to the attic, where the mementos of her Channel swim are stored. Beneath the dusty medals and crumbling newspaper clippings is a carefully wrapped pouch. It contains gold sovereigns, the award money from her achievement, enough to cover Velvet's fee. "Everyone should have a chance at a breathtaking piece of folly once in his life," she says.

This scene is the heart and soul of Velvet's story. It disproves the notion that women sabotage other women—and that mothers and daughters have an inborn enmity. Mrs. Brown doesn't rebel against the role of wife and mother. But she has known the pleasure of achievement—and she wants Velvet to know it too. In the film, to portray Mrs. Brown, Anne Revere wore almost no makeup. Her face is freckled and careworn. Yet she seems to glow—as unvarnished and radiant as truth itself.

Mrs. Brown embodies what writer Daniel Goleman terms "emotional intelligence." Although she excels at abstract thinking—she keeps the books for her husband's shop—she knows when to override reason with feeling. "You don't think like us," Velvet tells her mother. "You think back here." She pats the back of her head—the symbolic repository of empathy, intuition, and compassion.

After months of arduous training, Mi and Velvet reach the track—only to have their aspirations dashed. Velvet fires the jockey that Mi had hired for the race. The jockey lacked faith in Velvet's horse. She begs Mi to be the rider, but he refuses—until a long night of soul-searching restores the confidence he had lost. While Mi goes off to find himself, Velvet also looks within, realizing that she has more faith in her horse than Mi does. She is pleased when Mi tells her that he has overcome his fears. But while he was hesitating, she decided: she—not he—will ride the Pie.

Hair cropped and sporting pink-and-yellow silks, Velvet hurtles into the steeplechase—a whirlwind of dust, sweat, and hammering hooves. Oddly composed, she clings to the Pie, reassuring him of his greatness. All around her horses falter. Once boastful jockeys topple to the ground, their horses piling up around them. Every jump begets another crash. Accidents like the one that so spooked Mi are on the constant verge of happening.

The crowd thunders—louder than the hooves. When Velvet wins, it roars with astonishment—but not so loudly as it will roar later, when her gender is revealed.

According to the jacket notes on a recent edition of Enid Bagnold's novel, Velvet triumphed through "love, courage and the magical power of childhood dreams." I would have said chutzpah, cojones, and a hatred of injustice. Velvet rode better than most of the jockeys. Her expertise exposed the unfairness of excluding women. She proves that the rule is based on unfounded prejudice.

Both book and movie cunningly skirt an explicit confrontation over gender discrimination. Velvet slips off the horse after winning but before she leaves the track. This violates the rules, so regardless of her gender, she would have been disqualified. The movie hints that Velvet, like her mother, a former champion Channel swimmer, will savor her fifteen minutes of gender equality then retreat into the home. But the movie can't commit to this path. Velvet is only twelve years old, so shackling her immediately to her love interest, Mickey Rooney, is out of the question. She has six years to ponder a future like her mother's and perhaps find an alternative.

Immediately after the race, Velvet becomes a media phenomenon. Reporters from around the globe descend upon her village. They interview her friends, her parents, even her deranged younger brother, a bed wetter who wears his ant collection in a jar around his neck.

Lucrative offers pour in for Velvet and her horse. We know they're not a good idea because her mother hates them and they delight her father. "Do you want to go to America and act in the cinema?" Mr. Brown greedily inquires. Velvet is intrigued, but she ultimately declines. "Pie wouldn't understand," she explains. And "I'd sooner have that horse happy than go to heaven."

Here Velvet and Elizabeth part company. Like Velvet, Elizabeth loved animals. But her cherished pet, a chipmunk named Nibbles, did not apparently shrink from the limelight. After *National Velvet*, Simon & Schuster invited Elizabeth to write a book about him—*Nibbles and Me*—which she illustrated with her own pencil sketches. It chronicles the chipmunk's adventures, including his accidental swim in "Mummie's" toilet. But it is not all child's play. When Nibbles is fatally squished by a broken cage door, Elizabeth meditates on death, in a way that oddly foreshadows the losses she would later have to endure. Moving on, she says, does not imply forgetting: "I knew he would always live in my heart—and that another one would come to me . . . not to take his place, but to bring the same sense of love to me."

Sara Taylor kept young Elizabeth moving on—and on and on. She did not allow the girl to nap on her laurels. Sara wanted more for Elizabeth than a breathtaking piece of folly. She wanted fame and money and achievement. And if some of these things rubbed off on her, she would not protest.

3

1945–1950

BETWEEN 1945 AND 1950, Elizabeth blossomed, to a degree that few beings ever blossom, becoming, in the unlikely words of writer J. D. Salinger, "the most beautiful creature I have ever seen in my life." Under contract to MGM, she toiled faithfully in roles that didn't always further the cause of women but did establish the Taylor brand, which could later be put to more constructive use.

Not all her contract parts were milquetoast, however. Like *National Velvet*, *Cynthia* (1947) deals with conquering fear and getting back up on the proverbial horse. The film shows two women teaching a man how to be strong. Taylor plays Cynthia Bishop, a bookish teenager who as a child was plagued by life-threatening illnesses. These bouts so terrified her parents that that they cannot see that she has in adolescence become robust.

Before Cynthia was born, the Bishops were brave and had ambitions for themselves. But they use her nonexistent illness as a pretext to limit their lives. Cynthia's father is the greater coward. He lets his brother, a doctor, bully him and impose an absurd regimen on Cynthia: no apples, no fresh air, no singing. (Taylor actually sings in the movie, with a voice evocative of the ukulele-playing 1960s phenomenon, Tiny Tim.) When Cynthia can endure no more, she begs her mother for help, awakening Mrs. Bishop to her husband's irrationality. In defiance of his orders to lock up Cynthia when it's cold outside, she lets a handsome boy take her daughter to a dance in a rainstorm. To Mr. Bishop's astonishment, Cynthia does not die. She thrives—and her strength helps him rediscover the courage he lost.

In contrast, Mervyn LeRoy's *Little Women* (1949), adapted from Louisa May Alcott's 1869 novel, is a disappointment. In a head-turning blonde wig, Taylor portrays Amy March, one of four sisters who, along with their mother, tend the home fires in New England while their father serves in the Union army. "The novel is about female ambition," explains screenwriter Robin Swicord, who adapted a 1994 version directed by Gillian Armstrong that was scrupulously faithful to Alcott—a suffragist and abolitionist, whose feminist mother fiercely opposed the wearing of corsets. In the book, Jo wants to be a writer; Amy wants money; Beth wants a serene home, and only Meg wants a husband. But in LeRoy's movie, they all want husbands. And that's just about all he allows them to have.

In the MGM years, Taylor was often typecast as Daddy's pampered daughter. In *Father of the Bride*, she plays an upper-middle-class girl who will never work. She is traded from the hands of one man (her dad) into those of another (her husband). I find the movie vile, but happily, Taylor's part is minor. It stars Spencer Tracy, who opposes his daughter's request for a big church wedding. This might have been interesting if he had done this to protest religious hypocrisy or the treatment of brides as chattel. But he is simply cheap. He is also alcoholic—passing out drunk when he meets his future in-laws and worrying that his missteps will be blamed on booze. Nor does he realize that his actions often belie his words. Before committing full bore to the wedding—an insane orgy of *haute bourgeois* consumption—he tells his wife: "We're simple people. We live within our means."

In real life, however, Taylor could not have been more unlike the stereotype. Far from being Daddy's spoiled baby, Taylor supported her father, Francis, after World War II dealt a blow to his art business from which it never fully recovered. Taylor is known for having had intense, lifelong relationships with her gay male costars: Montgomery Clift, Rock Hudson, Roddy McDowall. But her first intense relationship with a gay man was with her own father, who was the longtime companion of Adrian, the MGM costume designer. On his birth certificate, Adrian had a first name—Gilbert—but perhaps in homage to his famous client, Garbo, he shed it. Adrian did not, however, shed his wife, actress Janet Gaynor, whom he married in 1939, when the studios, in a flurry of antigay housekeeping, married off all personnel who might be vulnerable to that era's equivalent of "outing." Like Adrian, Gaynor had some lavender issues to conceal. As one wag told writer Diana McLellan, "Janet's husband was Adrian . . . but her wife was Mary Martin."

From an early age, Taylor saw close-up the difference between the starry-eyed, media portrayal of marriage and the reality of her parents' business alliance. Francis had his own life and lovers; Sara, hers—including a brief affair in 1946 with Hungarian director Michael Curtiz, while he was making *Life with Father*, a movie that featured Elizabeth. But the Wedding-Industrial Complex, which arose in the 1950s alongside the Military-Industrial one, needed the shimmering myth of romantic love to unload its products. It needed to show people what to covet. And movie stars—whose lives were invented by studio publicists and embellished by fan magazines—made excellent teaching tools.

In the early years of Taylor's career, Sara and Elizabeth played the press—and, in particular, power brokers like Hedda Hopper and Louella Parsons—like a fine Stradivarius. If all the world loves a lover, mother and daughter made sure Elizabeth was perceived as such. In 1948, during the filming of *Julia Misbehaves*, Elizabeth met Glenn Davis—an all-American football player from West Point, so chisled and hunky that he seemed invented by central casting. During the filming of *Little Women*, she tantalized fans with their romance, announcing that they were "engaged to be engaged." But when Davis shipped off to the Korean War, her attention strayed—to a richer if somewhat less hunky prospect, William D. Pawley Jr. Upon his return, Davis squired Taylor to the 1949 Academy Awards, but shortly thereafter bolted, much to the delight of Pawley, who immediately proposed.

Despite his wealth, Pawley had many shortcomings. Poolside photos reveal that he was intensely hirsute, not unlike the Neanderthals who informed his views of women. Pawley believed that wives should stay home and be supported by their husbands. While in earshot of the fan magazines, Taylor claimed to think this was a swell idea. But later in 1949, when director George Stevens came calling, Taylor did what actors are trained to do. She revealed her character through action, swiftly giving Pawley the boot. The couple ended their engagement.

Stevens wanted Taylor for a project unlike anything he had previously directed. For over a decade, he had whipped up first-rate mainstream fare—comedies, musicals, and adventure stories—with stars like Fred Astaire, Ginger Rogers, Cary Grant, and Katharine Hepburn. He earned an Oscar nomination in 1943 for *The More the Merrier.* But World War II changed him. From 1943 to 1946, he volunteered to serve in the U.S. Army Signal Corps, where he headed a film unit that helped record the D-Day invasion. His unit bore witness to the horror of the Duben labor camp and the Dachau concentration camp—footage he later edited to prosecute war criminals at the Nuremberg Trials. After he returned to Hollywood, his films examined aspects of American society that, unchecked, might permit a dangerous slide from liberty to fascism. He explored class prejudice, racial bigotry, and the injustices of capitalism.

On its surface, the part that Stevens proposed—Angela Vickers in *A Place in the Sun*—was one at which Taylor had excelled: a rich girl. But he needed her to be something more: the "dream girl," every man's ideal, a woman so poised, wealthy, and desirable that a wrong-side-of-the-tracks fellow like George Eastman had to view her as unattainable. In a memo to William Meiklejohn, head of casting at Paramount, Stevens explained why Angela's perfection was essential to the plot. When George Eastman grasps that Angela Vickers is not beyond his reach, that he can, in fact, "have her, he is willing to commit murder and does to bring this about."

Angela's character, Stevens continued, is "the fundamental part of the machinery that goes to make the whole story work in relationship to its audience, and to keep the audience in a frame of mind that is sympathetic to all that it portrays."

For the role of Alice Tripp—the factory girl whom George impregnates—Stevens made a list of thirty actresses to consider. For Angela, he could think of only one: Taylor.

"Angela is not bound by the need to follow her father's grave conventions, because her own qualities would fit her for any world she chose to enter—be it rich or poor, bohemian or snobbish, pleasure-loving or serious," Stevens and screenwriters Michael Wilson and Harry Brown elaborated in a later memo. She rebels against the conformity and self-importance of her social circle. Not because she is a budding communist, but because such rules and rigidity "spoil and limit the world in which she alone is able to move with complete ease."

Did Taylor know what she was getting into? Kitty Kelley thinks not. MGM's Little Red School House did not serve its child actors well. In 1949, Kelley says, Taylor was barely educated and understood little beyond the price of a cashmere sweater. Taylor mostly took the part, Kelley suspects, to interrupt her servitude at MGM. But whatever propelled Taylor—instinct, intuition, maternal prodding, or escape—hardly matters. When the reviews came out, the Taylor brand soared. "Elizabeth Taylor is a joy to watch," Hollis Alpert wrote in the *Saturday Review of Literature.* "One had somehow never conceived of the glamorized creature as an actress."

Time magazine applauded Taylor's "tenderness," and the motivation her portrayal of Angela provided for George's behavior. But its reviewer was not blind to the film's underlying message, which involved reproductive rights. In its "boldest scene," *Time* writes, Shelley Winters, as Alice Tripp, "gropes, on the choked-up brink of tears, for a tactful way to ask a doctor for an abortion."

4

A Place in the Sun, 1951

Your problem is this: You have no money, no husband, and you don't dare tell your parents—perhaps—the truth. In relation to these difficulties, Miss Hamilton, I have but one duty—to see that you give birth to a healthy child. —Doctor Wyland addressing Alice Hamilton (precursor to Alice Tripp) in *A Place in the Sun.* (This draft by Michael Wilson is dated November 23, 1949.)

You understand that the foregoing suggestions are made merely in the hope that we can be helpful to you in salvaging what we realize is a very tense and dramatic scene. We must again say, however, that we cannot accept any suggestion of the <u>*subject*</u> *of abortion.* —Joseph I. Breen, Vice President and Director, Production Code Administration, in a letter to Luigi Luraschi, Director of Censorship, Paramount Pictures

BEFORE WE EXTEND our thumb and hitchhike with Montgomery Clift into the opening scene of *A Place in the Sun*, we need to look at the obstacle that George Stevens—or any director with integrity—faced in telling a nuanced story before 1968. Film is a mass medium. It can open the eyes of people to things that powerful institutions might prefer them to ignore. By the 1930s, one such institution, the Roman Catholic Church, realized that it needed to protect its flock from ideas that might challenge its primacy. And it did. For more than thirty years, a group of zealous American lay Catholics successfully connived to control and distort the content of American cinema.

Hollywood has never been a Protestant universe. In his book *An Empire of Their Own: How the Jews Invented Hollywood*, historian Neal Gabler explains how in the early twentieth century, recent immigrants, such as Taylor's boss, Louis B. Mayer, used films to invent an America so wholesome and "American" that it couldn't possibly exist. Then they colonized the imaginations of less recent immigrants—the moviegoing public—with what they made up. Mayer was no fan of communists or intellectuals, but he cared more about entertainment than ideology. In 1934, the Roman Catholic Legion of Decency and *The Commonweal*, a Roman Catholic publication, threatened the Motion Picture Producers and Distributors of America with a massive boycott of all Hollywood's so-called immoral movies. They organized not just Catholics, but churchgoers of many denominations. A boycott of this magnitude would never have been good for the studios, but during the Great Depression it would have destroyed them. To avert certain disaster, the MPPDA caved.

The censors instituted a set of guidelines known as the Production Code, or the Hays Code, after Will H. Hays, a former U.S. postmaster general and Republican National Committee chairman, who became president of the MPPDA in 1922. This was not a shining moment for Hollywood. A year earlier, comic actor Fatty Arbuckle had allegedly raped and murdered a woman while he was on a drinking spree in San Francisco. The tabloids had a field day—speculating on what foreign objects Arbuckle might have used to perpetrate the alleged rape. Although Arbuckle was later acquitted, the illegal boozing (Prohibition ran from 1920 until 1933) and sordid details led to an outcry against the film industry.

The Hays office was ostensibly secular; Hays was not a Roman Catholic. But his chief enforcer, Joseph I. Breen, was an ardent, Irish-American lay Catholic. Before 1934, Breen was also an open anti-Semite, making him an odd choice for a liaison with Hollywood. "These Jews seem to think of nothing but money making and sexual indulgence," Breen wrote to Reverend Wilfrid Parsons, S.J., the editor of the Jesuit magazine *America*, after a visit to Los Angeles in 1932. "People whose daily morals would not be tolerated in the toilet of a pest house hold the good jobs out there and wax fat on it. Ninety-five percent of these folks are Jews of an Eastern European lineage. They are, probably, the scum of the scum of the earth."

In 1932, however, Breen's slurs were not "eccentric utterances," wrote his biographer, Thomas Doherty. Such remarks—and worse—were commonplace among some gentiles until "Nazi genocide made outspoken anti-Semitism déclassé in polite conversation." Regardless of how Breen may have felt in private, he repudiated such prejudice in public, joining both the Hollywood Anti-Nazi League and the Committee of Catholics to Fight Anti-Semitism. And the Code itself forbade mocking all religions, not just Breen's.

The Production Code was written by Martin Quigley, Chicago-based editor of an obscure magazine about the movie industry, and Daniel Lord, a Jesuit, also from Chicago. Both were dedicated to preserving the foundations of a tidy, authoritarian society: the church, the government, and the family. (No, Lord is not a relative—though I did check since my extended family numbers several priests.) Lord and Quigley saw no need to regulate books or plays. If you were literate enough to read an idea-driven book or see a thought-provoking play, you likely were already lost—on the dangerous path to intellectual autonomy. But they feared the ubiquity—and persuasiveness—of movies.

The Code took a three-pronged approach. It forbade sympathetic portrayals of "sin"; it forbade ridicule of the law; and it required films to depict "the correct standards of life." Lord and Quigley never specified what those standards included, but they did detail what they didn't: nakedness, drug use, irreverence (to religion or the flag), adultery, sexual "perversion," and "miscegenation."

Although the Code has come to be associated with purging sex from movies, improper display of the U.S. flag was as severe an infraction as sodomy. In fairness, however, the Code had at least one good idea. Lord thought movies should be vague about criminal methods—lest they serve as a how-to manual for crooks.

Breen loved to put his fingerprints on all studio products,

even innocuous ones like *National Velvet.* In a letter to Mayer, he bristled at Velvet's allusion to puberty: "Please omit the action of Velvet tapping her chest and the line 'I am flat as a boy.'" He also objected to Velvet's sister rushing through grace after dinner: "This prayer must not be garbled but must be delivered straight." And he opposed showing Velvet in a locker room with "semi-nude jockeys." If the scene "is to be retained at all," he wrote, "all concerned will have to be fully clothed." Happily, Brown and Berman ignored the last directive, which would have made for an implausible locker room. They permitted some jockeys to change their shirts.

The Production Code Administration worked assiduously to remove all substance from *A Place in the Sun.* But Stevens overcame many of its efforts through the performance that he obtained from Taylor. The censors held sway over scripts. But *A Place in the Sun* conveyed more on screen than it did on paper because of all the nonverbal, primitive things that Taylor expressed, both subliminally and overtly.

Taylor spoke directly to our ancient aft-brain—our amygdala—the repository of love, hate, fear, and lust. On paper, in a love scene, having Angela whisper, "Tell Mama. Tell Mama all," would have seemed inane. In the film, the line, which was modified by Stevens during shooting, overrides our prefrontal cortex. Like a heat-seeking missile, it hones in on that aft-brain. Scan the brain of a viewer during that scene, and you would likely see the amygdala light up.

I doubt Stevens planned to short-circuit the audiences' prefrontal cortex. As an artist, he was operating from a place deep within his primal brain, accessing a palate of emotion, struggling to arouse certain feelings in the viewer. This was, of course, precisely what the Church feared—the power of music and image to provoke an emotional response. A power it knew well and drew upon in its rituals.

Color movies were commonplace in the 1940s. But for *A Place in the Sun*, Stevens wisely chose black-and-white. Censors see the world in polar opposites: good and evil, right and wrong, black and white. But the beauty of a black-and-white movie is that its frames are rarely all one tone or the other. Like life itself, the film unfolds in shades of gray.

To read the thick file of correspondence between Joseph I. Breen and Luigi Luraschi, Paramount's Director of Censorship,* you would think *A Place in the Sun* had only two characters, Alice Tripp and the doctor who refused to give her an abortion. In Theodore Dreiser's novel, the doctor is merely cold and unhelpful. But with Breen's guidance through several drafts of the script, the doctor becomes first callous and judgmental, then sanctimonious and punishing.

Happily, Shelley Winters, like Taylor, had the acting chops to convey what was going on in Alice's head, despite Breen's revisions. Her stricken eyes, her swallowed tears, and the catch in her voice alert us to her anguish. As does her bitter sarcasm when George asks what the doctor told her: "I'm going to have a healthy baby."

These nonverbal messages are key, because at one point Breen wanted Alice to fix her makeup, straighten her clothing, and deliver a lecture on the sociological implications of

* His real title.

unwed pregnancy—not something a bewildered girl would be likely to do. "We feel this story needs a voice for morality, between George and Alice," Breen wrote. "We think that, at about this page, either one of them, preferably Alice, should take some cognizance of the moral wrong of their predicament, as well as its social implications."

Breen also muzzled Clift: "George's line, 'I'll think of something,' together with the action indicated on page 65, will be unacceptable if it suggests George is thinking about consulting an abortionist. This entire element of contemplated abortion is unacceptable and could not be approved."

Breen seemingly wanted the actors to convey details about pregnancy to the audience through telepathy: "Please rewrite the following speech by Alice. 'The first night you came here . . . remember? You said I wouldn't have to worry. You said nothing would happen, remember?' Please omit the underlined words in Alice's line: 'Well—<u>it's happened</u>.' "

A rich girl in Alice's "predicament" would likely not have had a predicament. Such a girl's parents could at least afford to offer her a medical way out. But Breen strove to perpetuate Alice's misery, her tragic lack of options: "Please omit the following dialog—the last line being definitively suggestive of abortion: 'Oh. No change at all? Oh. Just the same? No, I haven't thought of anything yet.' "

Reading Breen's letters makes clear Stevens's directorial choices. He had to find symbolic ways to convey, for example, gnawing sexual desire because Breen would nix anything explicit. A neon sign—VICKERS—pulsates outside George's window; such a sign might well exist in a town where Angela's father is a captain of industry. Likewise, George's seduction of Alice is a tour de force of implication. Stevens conjures, through the urgent beat of a radio song, the moment when Alice's love and loneliness overcome her restraint. As *Time* magazine explained, "The players, barely visible as dim silhouettes, are no less Stevens' raw materials than the sounds, shadows and camera movements. And he molds and shapes them into probably the frankest, most provocative scene of its kind yet filmed in Hollywood."

Stevens doesn't cut nervously between actors. He plants the camera at a distance, and lingers. Still, his choices leave no confusion about which character we should observe. When, for instance, Alice tells George that she's "in trouble," we see the back of her head—the better to focus on George, whose turbulent feelings pass across his face like the shadows of clouds.

Stevens uses close-ups sparingly, heightening their effect. When Clift embraces Taylor, they fill the screen. We cannot turn away. She whispers, "Tell Mama. Tell Mama all."

When I first tried to watch *A Place in the Sun*, I couldn't view it all the way through. Stevens had gotten to me. I felt his characters' pain. I also felt powerless against a vague, inexorable evil to which only now have I been able to put a face: Joseph I. Breen's.

This has not made watching easier. When George stretches his meager budget to buy a tweed business suit, I always cry. I know he will arrive at his rich uncle's house and find all the other men in dinner jackets. When George meets Alice, I cry again. She is so unbearably innocent. I even sob when he meets Angela, because I see what Stevens wanted me to see: not a spoiled heiress, but George's other half.

By the time Stevens gets to the fatal boating accident, events race by like scenery past a speeding car. Stevens ratchets up the stress with sound. At George's murder trial, the loons, witness to the drowning, fill the courtroom with their eerie calls. In real life, a conviction is not a juggernaut. It is followed by appeal after time-consuming appeal. But this is a movie, and to maximize its drama, Stevens stages a swift death-row reunion with Angela—a scene that is as powerful as it is implausible. Through tears, Angela tells him, "I know I'll go on loving you for the rest of my life."

Some critics preferred the simplicity of Dreiser's novel. Capitalism is bad; the pregnant girl is good; the rich girl is whiney; and the guy is a cad—who, at the end, turns to religion for solace and repudiates his love.

In the film, George is tempted by religion. He even meets with a chaplain. But on the eve of his execution, when Angela enters his cell, all he sees is her scorching beauty. Angela is eros, not agape. She is pagan, not Christian. She mocks Breen—and the institutions that denied Alice a choice. Taylor has gotten to George as she has gotten to us: entering through our aft-brain and lodging in our soul.

5

1951–1955

A PLACE IN THE SUN wrapped in 1950, but it wasn't released until 1951, which left Elizabeth in an odd limbo. To the world at large, she was still the glossy bauble in *Father of the Bride* and its sequel, *Father's Little Dividend*. But under the tutelage of Clift, acclaimed for his method acting, Taylor's craft had evolved significantly. Stevens, too, had pushed her—once literally, off a rock into Lake Tahoe. He shot the film's summer holiday scenes there in the fall. The temperature rarely topped forty degrees. And when Taylor balked at taking an icy swim, Stevens gave her a shove.

Back in Beverly Hills, Taylor's mother, Sara, was less concerned with her growing credibility as an actress than with her marketability as a bride. Sara loved that millionaires were buzzing around her eligible daughter. She stoked the flames of the Wedding-Industrial Complex, making sure Hedda Hopper knew just how popular Elizabeth was. Soon, however, from the swarm of suitors, a special one arose: Nicky Hilton. And in a ceremony even more over-the-top than the one in *Father of the Bride*, he and Elizabeth were married.

The November 1950 issue of *Modern Screen* reveals the vast disconnect between real-life Hollywood and its engineered fantasy. In a five-page, stream-of-consciousness ramble, Hopper described the newlyweds on their honeymoon—from their love shack in Pebble Beach (a long way from *National Velvet*) to their voyage on the *Queen Elizabeth II.* Hopper dropped every imaginable name—from the Duke and Duchess of Windsor to composer Richard Rodgers to Butch, Elizabeth's recently deceased poodle.

"Nick's every bit as close to his dynamic dad as Elizabeth is to her doting mother," Hopper wrote. "Sara Taylor used to sigh to me, 'I always have to stay dressed up even when I go to bed the nights Elizabeth goes out.' Because no matter what time she came in, Liz raced right upstairs—usually bringing her dates along with her—to tell Mama all." The unfortunate word choice—"tell Mama all"—may have stuck with Hopper from an advance screening of *A Place in the Sun*. But I doubt she used it with deliberate irony. Irony seems outside her skill set. For example, during the filming of *A Place in the Sun*, with barely a gasp of incredulity, Hopper reported plans for a musical version of Dreiser's novel—with Bing Crosby as the murderer.

Unfortunately, two months into the marriage, Elizabeth did have much to tell Mama—about Nicky clobbering her. And Sara faced a daunting choice—between Hilton's millions and her daughter's well-being. Sara chose her daughter, and Elizabeth and Hilton divorced.

Elizabeth was not single for long. Disillusioned with young rakes like Hilton, she fell for an older one, actor Michael Wilding, twenty years her senior. They married in London in 1952. Her fans were thrilled, and all had hopes for "happily ever after." Or nearly all. Actress Marlene Dietrich, an ex-lover of Wilding, despised Taylor and was bitter about the marriage, which she attributed to cheap physical attraction. "It must be those huge breasts of hers," Dietrich told her daughter, Maria Riva. "He likes them to dangle in his face."

Wilding, some say, married Taylor to advance his lagging career—or at least get a toehold in the United States. But if so, the strategy failed. MGM gave him a few parts, including a painful paring with Joan Crawford in *Torch Song* in 1953. But by 1955, the Wildings had two sons, Michael Howard, born in 1953, and Christopher Edward, who arrived two years later. And the role Wilding mostly played was dad.

After *A Place in the Sun*, Elizabeth's value skyrocketed—so high that it seemed unlikely ever to go down. But between 1952 and 1956, MGM managed to slow its climb, by casting her in a series of duds, including *Elephant Walk*, *Love Is Better than Ever*, *Ivanhoe*, *Beau Brummell*, and *Rhapsody*, a film that Elizabeth herself said "should never have been made by me or anybody else."

Taylor's worst film from this period had the best pedigree: *The Last Time I Saw Paris*, "inspired" by F. Scott Fitzgerald's splendid short story "Babylon Revisited." "Inspired" is the word Hollywood uses when it buys a work and makes it into something altogether different. This is not always bad; the film versions of *National Velvet* and *A Place in the Sun* were very strong. This was not the case with *The Last Time I Saw Paris*.

Fitzgerald wrote a moral tale about alcoholism. It deals with a self-pitying narcissist who goes on a protracted bender in Paris. There he mistreats his wife and, while drunk, locks her out of their house during a blizzard. As in *Cynthia*, where cold air, not germs, cause pneumonia, the wife gets sick and dies. In the movie, Taylor plays the wife, Helen; Van Johnson, the lush, Charles. And the blizzard in which Charles, intoxicated, gurgles while Helen pounds the front door, is unintentionally hilarious. Yet in Fitzgerald's story, the lush is justifiably punished. His dead wife's family takes his child away. The story has a moral core. Richard Brooks, who directed the film and also served as one of its screenwriters, throws out that core—and replaces it with hokum. Charles, newly contrite and occasionally sober, gets to keep the child *whose mother he killed*.

Brooks's blithe evisceration of "Babylon Revisited" was a harbinger of worse to come. In a few years, he would get his bowdlerizing mitts on Tennessee Williams's *Cat on a Hot Tin Roof*, an important Broadway play about homosexuality. And quicker than you can say "Lord Alfred Douglas," he would hack the homo from the sexuality. He landed a fine cast for this film, including Taylor, and they all performed well—tragically, however, in the service of an inane plot contrived to appease the Production Code Administration.

In 1955, however, *Cat* was far down the road. The Taylor brand was languishing—as was Taylor's marriage. She needed a film worthy of her gifts. She needed a director who understood her, and who would put her strengths to a higher purpose. She needed George Stevens.

And thanks to Rock Hudson, she got him—as well as a break from her contract with MGM. Stevens had offered Hudson the male lead in *Giant*—a Warner Brothers film that was as strapping and ambitious as the six-foot-five-inch actor himself. For the female lead, Stevens had wanted Grace Kelly, who turned down the part to marry Prince Rainier of Monaco. Uncertain how to proceed, Stevens asked Hudson whom he pictured in the role of Hudson's character's wife. Hudson requested Taylor. So in May 1955, Taylor, Hudson, Stevens, and a sexually cryptic newcomer, James Dean, struck out for the punishing flats of Marfa, Texas—a world apart from the glitz of Hollywood—where they would create something extraordinary.

6

Giant, 1956

You gentlemen date back a hundred thousand years. You ought to be wearing leopard skins and carrying clubs. Politics? Business? What is so masculine about a conversation that a woman can't enter into it?

—Elizabeth Taylor as Leslie Lynnton Benedict in *Giant*

If George Stevens had deliberately set out to make a feminist propaganda film, he could not have achieved a greater success than he did with *Giant*. The movie is based on Edna Ferber's sprawling novel of the same name—only nominally a portrait of Texas, where the book is set, and more a celebration of its formidable heroine, Leslie Lynnton Benedict, who with cajoling words and gentle force tames a brutal frontier. Leslie also fights discrimination against Mexican immigrants, making the film as timely today as when it came out in 1956.

According to Albert Sindlinger, a market researcher whose firm analyzed film attendance in the 1950s, *Giant* reversed a five-year box-office downturn, "bringing back many people—especially women—who had nearly given up the movie habit all together."

As the story moves from the 1930s to the 1950s, *Giant* exalts what feminists of the 1970s termed "essentialist" values. Smart and well schooled, Leslie demonstrates that higher education need not transform a woman into a parody of a man. Leslie owns her beauty—for that matter, she owns *Taylor's* beauty—and displays it to its best advantage. But she is far from a narcissist. In an early scene that defines her character, Leslie overcomes heat, dirt, fatigue, and the racial bigotry of her husband to secure medical care for a sick Mexican child. Leslie embodies the values of the right brain: empathy, compassion, and a belief in social justice. Over time, she introduces these values to the left-brained (and occasionally no-brained) inhabitants of the Lone Star state.

Feminism and social justice have always been closely linked. Susan B. Anthony and Elizabeth Cady Stanton, founding mothers of American feminism, were both abolitionists. (Though Stanton was not exactly thrilled when freed black men got the vote before women.) In the 1950s and '60s, a commitment to social justice often prefigured an involvement with feminism. As writer Sara Evans observes in *Personal Politics: The Roots of Women's Liberation in the Civil Rights Movement and the New Left*, many women became feminists after fighting for racial justice in the American South: "There they found the inner-strength to explore the meaning of equality and an ideology that beckoned them to do so."

In *Giant*, Leslie is at one with the natural world. As in *National Velvet*, Taylor portrays a horsewoman who seems to collude with her mount, rather than force it into submission. We first see her in the rolling Maryland countryside, galloping, as the natives say, "to hounds." Meanwhile, another sort of horse—a clanging iron one—rolls into the nearby train station. It carries Bick Benedict, a Texas cattle baron, portrayed with a swagger by Hudson. He has traveled east from Reata, his two-and-a-half-million-acre ranch, to purchase the horse Leslie rides, War Winds, from Leslie's father, Dr. Lynnton. Driving from the depot to the Lynnton home, Bick glimpses Leslie atop the midnight-colored stallion. Flushed, radiant, she fixes him with those violet eyes. "That sure is a beautiful animal," he blurts.

Of course, Bick falls in love with Leslie—she's Elizabeth Taylor. But she also represents what he himself lacks: tenderness, education, and feminine values. In an instant, the audience grasps what it takes Bick a three-and-a-quarter-hour movie to realize: Leslie is Bick's other half.

Aside from his looks—and the two and a half million acres—what Leslie initially sees in Bick is less clear. When, after a whirlwind courtship, Leslie arrives at Reata, she has what my friend Lindsay calls her *Rebecca* moment, after Alfred Hitchcock's 1940 psychological thriller. Reata is not the lush, Edenic East Coast countryside of Leslie's childhood. It is a flat, featureless desert: arid, harsh, pockmarked with tumbleweeds. Nor is Leslie allowed to take her rightful place at the head of Bick's household. Another woman is in charge: one who, like the deranged Mrs. Danvers in *Rebecca*, is set on destroying the new woman in the house.

This charmer is Bick's sister Luz, a barrel-chested oaf who seems to have no right brain at all. Instead of challenging the fact that men rule the roost in a frontier culture, Luz tries to make herself more mannish than the men. As portrayed by Mercedes McCambridge, Luz has the grace of a buffalo at a debutante ball. She is bossy, the way Stalin, Ceauşescu, and Pol Pot were bossy, but because she lacks the top job in a dictatorship, she satisfies her urge to dominate through torture by abusing animals. She won't even soften in private; she clomps around the house in her spurs.

But Luz cannot annihilate Leslie. As determined to ease suffering as Luz is to cause it, Leslie parries Luz's blows, emerging stronger. Frustrated, Luz hops on War Winds and attempts to do to him what she would like to do to Leslie: gouge his sides with those spurs until he submits. But War Winds has other plans. He bucks her off with sufficient force to cause a fatal accident. Carried back to the parlor in Reata, Luz dies with her boots on, spurs conspicuously shredding the leather sofa.

Meanwhile, away from the ranch, Jett Rink, Bick's dirt-poor hired hand, drives Leslie to the squalid village where Bick's Mexican workers live. Rink, memorably portrayed by James Dean, simmers in class resentment, which takes the form of hunching, mumbling, and skirting eye contact. He had intended to annoy Bick and shock Leslie by showing her the encampment. Instead, Leslie finds—and saves—a dying child, forcing the white ranchers' physician to tend to him.

Jett Rink is patterned after Glenn Herbert McCarthy, a famously vulgar, up-from-nowhere wildcatter who used his oil riches to found Houston's Shamrock Hotel. To the degree that Ferber's novel was a satire on real people, Texans hated it. Ferber, however, could not have cared less. Brought up in a midwestern Jewish family, she worked insanely hard to gain recognition as a writer in Manhattan. And she succeeded: co-writing plays with George S. Kaufman, fraternizing with Dorothy Parker at the Algonquin Hotel, and winning the 1924 Pulitzer Prize for her novel *So Big.* Unfortunately, she was better at gaining recognition than at actual writing—which is why few people know her books today.

"Reading *Giant* for a second time was a painful, if not outright excruciating experience," *Washington Post* book critic Jonathan Yardley wrote when *Giant* was reissued in 2006, and, as usual, Yardley is right. "Aspiring to irony, Ferber rarely rises above sarcasm. Her prose is almost entirely lacking in grace or rhythm." Happily, however, "the movie is so much better than the book as to seem an almost entirely different piece of work."

In the same way that Stevens took Dreiser's anticapitalist screed and made it into a multi-Kleenex blockbuster, he took Ferber's cartoon and made it into a masterpiece. Credit must also go to screenwriters Fred Guiol and Ivan Moffat, for, among other things, placing the climax near the end of the movie instead of at its beginning. And to cinematographer William C. Mellor, for capturing the cruel splendor of the sun-bleached West.

Often, when Taylor's character is allied with nature, nature is all-powerful. In *Giant*, nature is not easily tamed, and human efforts are often so ineffectual as to be comical. We see this when Leslie first glimpses Reata: a proper Victorian house plopped down in the dusty emptiness, like a spaceship on Mars. And we see it at the movie's climax—a fierce thunderstorm, whose torrents mirror the human clash below.

Leslie doesn't earn her feminist stripes in a single scene, but over time. Her ultimate victory is to raise a feminist son, who will impart her values to the next generation. She doesn't defy; she subverts. Yet in a speech whose overt feminism is startling for a mid-1950s movie, she makes clear that she wants no part of a culture that demeans women. Nor is it words alone that carry the scene; it is Stevens's direction and Taylor's acting.

After dinner at Reata, that great white elephant of a house, the men and women segregate themselves. Until one night when Leslie—wrapped in a Greek chiton, equal parts Aphrodite and Athena—dares to invade the masculine enclave.

"You'll be bored, honey," Bick says, when she won't go away. "We're talking politics."

"You married me in Washington, darling. I lived next door to politics. Please do go on."

But Bick refuses: "This is men's stuff."

"Men's stuff?" Leslie explodes. "Lord, have mercy! Set up my spinning wheel, girls. I'll join the harem section in a minute."

The men, who had been indifferent, suddenly glower. Stevens focuses on their faces, not Leslie's. When she accuses them of behaving like cavemen, they look as if they'd like to use their clubs on her.

"Leslie, you're tired," Bick says, to silence her.

And she *is* tired: of his patronizing, his misogyny, his contempt.

With resignation—but not in defeat—she walks to the base of the massive staircase, pausing to study the men, who struggle to ignore her. She has never looked wiser, more self-possessed, or more mature—despite their little-boy efforts to infantilize her. "That's right," she says, speaking with care. "Send the children on up to bed so the grown-ups can talk."

That night, of course, Bick and Leslie fight. But they make up. Because Leslie holds a trump: She is pregnant with their child—a son—who, as yet unbeknownst to Bick, will break open his narrow, prejudiced, masculine world.

Giant exploded gender stereotypes before this was fashionable. Bick expects their son, Jordan Benedict III, scion of the Benedict cattle empire, to adore horseback riding. But when he gives the boy a pony, "Jordy" screams—preferring quiet play with his plastic doctor kit. Leslie supports her son's desire to study medicine. But she, too, has her preconceptions challenged—when one of their daughters, whom Leslie had planned to send to a fancy girls' school, prefers to study ranching at Texas A&M. (The other daughter rebels in a more traditional fashion: falling for a no-good man.)

The greatest conflict hanging over Texas—and over all of America in the 1950s—was the fight for civil rights, which *Giant*'s roller-coaster climax tackles. In the context of the movie, the civil rights struggle is an extension of the feminist struggle. Leslie is committed to social justice. When she forced the white ranchers' doctor to save a dying Mexican child, she made this clear. She also imbued Jordy with her core values, and he carries on Leslie's fight. After an Ivy League medical education, he returns to the border states to provide health care to migrant workers and the poor. And he marries a Mexican woman, a bold act in the 1950s—one whose depiction on screen, before *Giant*, had been outlawed by the Production Code. (Interracial marriage remained illegal in many southern states, including Texas, until 1967, when the Supreme Court pronounced the proscription unconstitutional.)

The film sets up Jett Rink as Jordy's polar opposite. At the beginning of the movie, Stevens tempts us to root for Rink. He grew up broke, and his struggles toward self-betterment—memorizing vocabulary and learning to make tea—are poignant. But when he strikes oil and becomes a billionaire, he builds an absurdly lavish hotel and orders its staff to refuse service to nonwhite people. He props himself up by tearing down others—whole races of them.

Rink and Jordy clash at the black-tie opening of Rink's hotel—which the Benedicts (also newly oil-rich) have been pressured to attend. Jordy expects the event to annoy him—and regrets agreeing to attend—but when the hotel beauty salon bars his wife, Juana, he hits the roof. The beautician is baffled by his anger: "She should have gone to Sanchez' place, where they do her people."

Too furious to notice the thunderstorm through which he has slogged, Jordy, dripping, confronts Rink at the dinner in Rink's honor. Portrayed with passion by Dennis Hopper, Jordy is a small, clenched bundle of indignation in a ballroom full of rangy, tuxedo-clad cowboys—the state's petroleum elite. Rink sneers; he loathes Jordy's education, idealism, and last name. He taunts Jordy about "marrying a squaw." Then he orders his goons to hold Jordy back, so that he can avenge years of class resentment, throwing a punch to flatten the rich boy. Leslie winces when Jordy is struck; but she is proud that her son stood up to injustice. Bick, however, shamed, leaps to defend the Benedict family honor—not to demand respect for Jordy's wife.

Bick prides himself on being open-minded. But later, when he counsels Jordy to expect confrontation—that it comes with "marrying in that direction"—he exposes his prejudice. Bick is just a less-crude version of Rink. On the edge of tears, Jordy begs his father to hear what he has said—and to fight against the bigotry in his heart.

At Sarge's Diner, a roadside dump on the drive back to Reata, Jordy's message sinks in. Sarge, the loutish white owner, grudgingly serves Leslie, Juana, Bick, and Bick's biracial grandson. But when a Mexican couple sits down, Sarge evicts them. And Bick raises his fists—not for family honor or personal pride, but for something larger—racial justice—in which before this moment he had only superficially believed.

Bick does not prevail. Sarge decks him; he crashes into a stack of dishes and topples to the floor. But in Leslie's eyes, he is victorious. He has experienced a flicker of empathy. She has also triumphed. Her values don't just reside in the Benedict children; they have taken root in her husband as well: "After a hundred years, the Benedict family is really a success."

Giant "depicts the erosion of sexual stereotyping," critic Peter Biskind writes in *Seeing Is Believing: How Hollywood Taught Us to Stop Worrying and Love the Fifties*. "Leslie is more assertive, more a man than her mother back in Maryland, and she feminizes Bick, sees to it that he becomes more a woman than his father." In 1956—the same year that *Rebel Without a Cause* blamed teenage delinquency on fathers who wear aprons—this itself was an achievement.

But Stevens doesn't just break down gender polarities. He implies that the innate values of women are nobler than those of men. He takes Leslie's world—the world of women—and connects it to the "aggregate of pluralist values," the "highest aspirations" toward which a civilization can strive: "tolerance, compromise, flexibility, and civility," Biskind writes. He does this through Leslie's commitment to social justice. In *Giant*, Biskind asserts, "woman's world comes to be equated with nothing less than culture itself."

7

1956–1959

As you can imagine, Warner Brothers did not sell *Giant* as a feminist call to arms. It sold the film as a steamy love triangle—misrepresenting, often comically, the content of scenes. The ad campaign used "subliminal seduction," a then-trendy technique for selling products by stealthily linking them to sex. The studio ran a half-page ad with three big pictures. In the first, Hudson, valiantly heterosexual, gazes longingly at Taylor. The caption: "Bick Benedict, owning so much except the one part of Leslie's life that is no part of his."

The ad then shows Dean, shirt unbuttoned to the waist, oozing intensity, and Taylor *on her knees* before him. Although they are technically chaste, their positions hint at an act that would violate the Production Code. The caption: "Jett Rink, the outsider—and Leslie, wealthy and beautiful."

The last frame shows Dean leering at Taylor as if she were a hamburger and he had missed lunch. The caption: "Jett Rink's shack. No one has ever set foot in it—and then, suddenly, Leslie." The last picture is the most distorted. Far from depicting a sweaty, libidinous tryst, the actual scene is prim and tender. To show Leslie that he is not a brute, Jett struggles to get everything right as he makes her a cup of tea. His actions are a perfect metaphor for the feminization of the West.

Unlike the ad, with its inadvertent comedy, tragedy hung over the production, as it would soon over Taylor's life. On September 30, 1955, shortly before the film was due to wrap, Dean fatally crashed his Porsche 550 Spyder on his way to a road race in Salinas, California. Dean and Hudson had avoided each other during filming; Hudson, some biographers theorize, was miffed when Dean rebuffed his advances. But Taylor forged close platonic relationships with both men. When she learned of the accident, she collapsed. Stevens was furious; Taylor's histrionics were delaying his movie. Stevens thought Dean had been addicted to risk; he almost expected Dean to meet a premature demise. Challenge death often enough, and death is likely to prevail. But Taylor had to be hospitalized—sickened, her internist wrote, by both grief and "the extreme mental duress she was put under by the director." Her final performances, however, proved worth the wait. Although she herself did not earn an Academy Award for *Giant*, she helped Stevens win his second.

Happily, when Taylor returned to Los Angeles, Wilding was no longer unemployed. MGM gave the forty-three-year-old actor a part, though not one suited to his maturity and gravitas. Outfitted in tights and ballet shoes, the uniform of a fairytale prince, he skipped and hopped through *The Glass Slipper*, a musical version of *Cinderella*.

After Taylor scored a success for a rival studio, MGM seemed oddly determined to drag her down—as it had done after *A Place in the Sun.* It foisted a lemon of a script upon her: *Raintree County,* a cheap reworking of *Gone with the Wind* set in the North. Taylor's character, Susanna, was supposed to resemble Scarlett O'Hara, except that, as the part was written, the character had neither Scarlett's wit nor her cunning nor her survival instinct. She had Scarlett's beauty, but this was wasted without Scarlett's genius for using it to manipulate men. As Leslie Benedict in *Giant,* Taylor had delivered an eloquent plea for racial justice. By contrast, in *Raintree County,* Taylor is forced to portray a self-destructive bigot. Her character goes nuts—babbling, gurgling, and, ultimately, drowning herself—from fear that she has "Negro blood."

At least MGM cast Taylor opposite her friend Montgomery Clift—fresh from a celebrated performance in *From Here to Eternity.* But this, too, would lead to tragedy. On May 12, 1956, Taylor and Wilding invited a few friends to their Benedict Canyon house for dinner. The guests included Rock Hudson and his wife, Phyllis Gates (former secretary to Hudson's agent, whom Hudson had married to banish rumors about his sexuality). She also invited Clift and the actor Kevin McCarthy, who was visiting Los Angeles to work on a TV program. Clift and McCarthy had been friends since 1941, when they met in New York at the Actors Studio.

During the filming of *Raintree County,* Taylor lived in a modernist house high on Beverly Estates Drive, which snakes up from the floor of Benedict Canyon—a rustic, wooded enclave adjacent to Beverly Hills. Even today, with abundant streetlights, smooth pavement, and a house on every lot, the street is treacherous at night. In 1956, the street was pitch-dark, pothole-ridden, and virtually uninhabited.

Clift's biographer, Patricia Bosworth, wrote that Clift regularly mixed booze with prescription drugs while shooting *Raintree County.* But when I interviewed McCarthy in Los Angeles, he insisted that Clift and he had "gone on the wagon" that day.

The dinner, he recalled, was unremarkable, except that Wilding had a sore back and spent the night horizontal on a couch. At about ten thirty P.M., McCarthy excused himself. He had to travel to Berkeley, California, early the next morning. Clift knew the canyon even less well than McCarthy, so Clift left with McCarthy, planning to follow him down the hill.

The two men had rented identical cars—brown-and-white, four-door Chevrolets. As McCarthy eased through the first hairpin turn, he was jolted alert. Clift had hung back, then surged forward. That daredevil, McCarthy thought. "He's trying to tickle my bumper." So McCarthy sped up, zipping through another sharp curve. But suddenly, he recalled, "I didn't see his lights anymore. I thought, Now what the hell has he done? Gone out to take a leak?"

Fear replaced annoyance. In the rearview mirror, McCarthy saw headlights—erratic flickers—as if a car were careening from object to object. He raced back up the hill: "I saw Monty's car. The lights were on. The motor was racing."

McCarthy ran to turn off the ignition. The doors were mangled, jammed. Because he couldn't see a driver, McCarthy assumed Clift had been thrown clear. But when he reached through a shattered side window to turn the key, he saw Clift—bloody, crushed—beneath the level of the dashboard.

"Even now it hurts to talk about it," he remembered decades later. "It brings tears to my eyes. I thought: What do I do? I can't just leave him here. But I have to leave him here—to get help."

McCarthy zoomed to the Wilding residence. "Get an ambulance!" he shouted when Wilding opened the door. "Monty's been in an accident." While Wilding barked details into the telephone, McCarthy and Taylor barreled down to Clift.

"He was conscious," McCarthy said. "Sort of groaning—going, mrrrrr, mrrrrr. And I froze." But Taylor rushed to him. She tugged and pounded on the doors, and when they wouldn't budge, she climbed through a rear window—indifferent to the grease, blood, and dust on what McCarthy recalled had been her white silk dress. As Taylor cradled Clift's head, he made that "mrrrrr" noise again. He was choking. His front teeth had been dislodged by the impact and were now stuck in his throat. Without hesitating, Taylor reached into his mouth and pulled them out. She saved his life.

"Liz was so strong," McCarthy said. "Like one of those pioneer women. Like you read about. Like . . . like—"

Like Leslie Benedict in *Giant*? I suggested.

"Yes!" He agreed. "In so many ways."

Rex Kennamer, Clift's doctor, arrived first at the scene. Even at death's door, Clift never forgot his manners. He politely introduced Kennamer to Taylor. No sooner had she said hello than she was again forced to harden into Leslie Benedict.

Behind the ambulance came the press, jockeying for a gruesome shot of Clift. "Get those goddamned cameras out of here!" Taylor shouted, covering his face with her hands. Then, in a voice that sent the photographers scrambling, she added, "Or I'll make sure you never work in Hollywood again."

Although Clift's nose was broken, his face bandaged, and his smashed jaw wired shut, he survived. In occasional upbeat moments he even sipped martinis through a straw. Such moments, however, were few and far between—for both him and Taylor. Between Clift's accident and Dean's death, Taylor was badly in need of solace. She grieved, too, for her marriage to Wilding, which was past resuscitation. In such a state, what could be more normal than to seek comfort, and, if one looked like Taylor, to find it? During this time, biographers link her first with singer Frank Sinatra, then with cinematographer Kevin McClory, who had worked as a unit director on *Around the World in 80 Days*, producer Mike Todd's latest movie.

McClory, however, made a very big mistake. He introduced Taylor to Todd. Within hours of their meeting, Todd, the cigar-chomping Broadway impresario turned Hollywood *macher*, had fallen in love. Never mind that she was still married to Wilding, Todd courted her lavishly. He courted her on location in Kentucky, where *Raintree County* was shooting. He courted her with presents—sparkling, eye-catching objects—a Cartier emerald bracelet, a $30,000 black pearl ring, and, eventually, a 24.9-carat diamond engagement ring.

In November 1956, Taylor filed for divorce from Wilding.

She became Mrs. Michael Todd in February 1957 in Acapulco, Mexico. Having become pregnant by Todd in late 1956, Taylor needed a speedy Mexican divorce—and Wilding, for $200,000 and proceeds from the sale of the Benedict Canyon house, was willing to accommodate. He left Mexico when the divorce was final—two days before the wedding.

Wilding retreated to London to avoid journalists, who nevertheless tracked him down. Beleaguered yet classy, he wished the couple well, hoping Taylor would find with Todd what she had been unable to find with him. "They are," he observed, "two of a kind."

Wilding may have meant the remark disparagingly, as a comment on their emotional rapaciousness. But the fact was, Todd and Taylor had much in common professionally. They approached their movie work in a similar way. Each aspired to the same goal: overriding a viewer's logical left brain by engaging his or her intuitive right—or better yet, striking the mother lode of emotion: the reptile brain.

Taylor moved toward this instinctively. As directed by Stevens in *A Place in the Sun*, she enflamed the screen with unambiguously grown-up desire—using words that the left brain would dismiss as baby talk: "Tell Mama. Tell Mama all." Because he worked behind the scenes and not in front of an audience, Todd approached this goal more deliberately and methodically—by investing in technologies to expand the sensory limits of film. At the 1939 World's Fair, Todd, then a Broadway producer, met Fred Waller, inventor of a three-camera, wraparound screening system that plunged viewers into a projected world. Captivated, Todd invested in the system, christened it Cinerama, and in 1952, brought out *This Is Cinerama*—a movie to show what the technology could do. Highlighted by a harrowing ride on the Coney Island roller coaster, the movie anticipated the immersiveness of virtual reality.

Buoyed by this success, Todd pushed harder, funding what he hoped would be another breakthrough, Smell-O-Vision, which recognized the emotional power of scent. Taylor, too, understood this power; and perhaps Todd's dream—the dream of Smell-O-Vision—inspired her in later years to found a perfume empire, one of whose cornerstone fragrances is named Passion.

This is not a glib connection. An appreciation of smell sets its possessors apart; it suggests a heightened receptivity to sensual information. The base of most perfumes is musk, a secretion from abdominal glands in the male musk deer. This substance contains a potent sexual allure—a chemical magnet, whose very molecules must enter our bodies for us to sense them. Smell often triggers a violent response. Bad smells repel us, protecting us from, for example, spoiled food. Beguiling smells seduce us. They tickle the primitive brain. Often they override judgment. "The nose really is a sex organ," playwright Tony Kushner wrote in *Angels in America*, winner of the 1993 Pulitzer Prize for Drama. Smelling "is desiring."

The olfactory sense does not work like vision, hearing, or touch. To perceive an aroma, receptors in the nose must come in contact with actual bits of the aroma's source. Smell is a comingling of substances, as is sex. "We have five senses," Kushner continued. "But only two that go beyond the boundaries . . . of ourselves. When you look at someone, it's just bouncing light, or when you hear them, it's just sound waves vibrating air, or touch is just nerve endings tingling." But smell is made "of the molecules of what you're smelling."

Kushner's explanation is not only scientifically accurate but also part of a memorable seduction scene. Taylor and Todd may not have known how smell worked—scientists continue to study the process—but they understood its power, and they knew that skilled technicians could help them exploit it. To realize his idea, Todd worked with top engineers. To formulate her scents, Taylor hired preeminent chemists.

Smell-O-Vision should not be confused with Odorama, the facetious scratch-and-sniff card that director John Waters created for his 1981 movie, *Polyester.* Smell-O-Vision involved scent canisters on a turntable that was synchronized with a projector so that odors would be released at key points in a film. It also featured a blower to flush scents from the theater before introducing new ones. Smell-O-Vision was precise and technically sophisticated. To manufacture it, the Todd organization engaged the Belock Instrument Corporation, a Long Island–based defense contractor that built guidance-and-control systems for the Atlas and Polaris missiles.

Todd's tragic, premature death in March 1958 prevented him from bringing Smell-O-Vision to market. The owner of a rival theater chain, Walter Reade Jr., got there first with a poorly thought-out system called AromaRama, whose very name mocked Todd's groundbreaking Cinerama. Reade chose *Behind the Great Wall*, a travelogue about then-communist

China, to demonstrate his device. Its slogan was "*You must breathe it to believe it.*"

Unfortunately, AromaRama lacked a means to clear a room of odors before adding new ones. It pumped smells willy-nilly into the audience, one on top of the other. Sometimes its mistakes were funny. "At one point, the audience distinctly smells grass in the middle of the Gobi Desert," *Time* magazine wrote. Similarly, an "old pine grove in Peking" smells like "a subway rest room on disinfectant day." Mostly, though, the layered scents sickened viewers, inflaming allergies and lodging in clothes.

When Smell-O-Vision debuted a month later, it worked without a hitch: no missed cues or layered stenches. But this didn't matter. Reade had already discredited the concept.

On November 4, 1957, Todd was still very much alive, and *Life* magazine offered a rare peek inside the Taylor-Todd household. On the cover, Taylor looks radiant: indifferent to the camera, absorbed by her three-month-old daughter, Liza Todd. Inside the magazine, she and Todd roughhouse with Michael and Christopher Wilding. Although Taylor's makeup is light and her clothing casual, she is far from unadorned. The diamond on her left hand is as big as her daughter's head.

On the eve of all her marriages—to Hilton, Wilding, and now Todd—Taylor professed a deep yearning to ditch acting for motherhood. The yearning, however, never got in the way of her work. On March 2, 1958, she returned to MGM to portray Maggie the Cat in Richard Brooks's bizarre, craven replica of Tennessee Williams's *Cat on* a *Hot Tin Roof.*

In the play, Brick, Maggie's husband, is explicitly gay. He won't sleep with Maggie because he is in love with his dead best friend, Skipper. In the movie, Brick avoids Maggie for no reason—particularly in light of Taylor's beauty and what Williams called her engaging "rocket tits." "Tenn always joked that even *he* would have been able to 'bounce the springs' a few times with Taylor's Maggie," James Grissom, author of *Follies of God*, told me. "He didn't feel anyone could understand Brick's revulsion with the obligation."

However, by the time MGM made *Cat on a Hot Tin Roof*, Williams was just "cashing checks," Grissom said. He didn't involve himself artistically in adaptations of his work. The studio had paid him $450,000 for the rights—which presumably included the right to mangle his plot and eliminate his characters' motivations. Nevertheless, when the film came out, Williams flipped. "He advised strangers against seeing the film," Meade Roberts, a friend of Williams, told writer C. David Heymann. He would stand outside movie theaters, trying to block people from entering.

If Taylor had reservations about the bastardized script, she did not express them. And soon she would find herself in no position to turn down work. On March 21, 1958—barely three weeks into the movie—Mike Todd's private plane, ironically named the *Lucky Liz*, crashed in New Mexico, killing the man she had called the "love of my life." Taylor was devastated, by grief of course, but also, because she had chosen not to fly with Todd, by survivor's guilt.

If ever there were a time to retreat and heal, this was it. But then Taylor made a startling discovery: Todd had left her no financial cushion. The accoutrements of their sumptuous life were almost entirely leased. Todd had a mere $250,000 in the bank. Alone, bereft, Taylor had three children to support. So she mourned—deeply and passionately—for one month and three days. Then she went back to work. In the first scene she filmed after Todd's death, she spoke an especially resonant line: "I know what it's like to lose someone you love."

Far more than any direction she received from Brooks, grief intensified Taylor's performance—sadly wasted on the gutted script. Grief exposes vulnerabilities. It sharpens feelings. It unlocks doors to the heart. But grief also clouds judgment. And it cries out constantly for balm—without much concern for where the balm is coming from.

Like Taylor, Todd's closest male friend, Eddie Fisher, was also in mourning. He, too, needed comfort—which his wife, perky actress Debbie Reynolds, apparently declined to provide. To console Taylor in her grief, Fisher rushed to her side. And soon, as Carrie Fisher, his daughter, later wrote, he moved "to her front." This prevented his returning to Reynolds. "America's Sweethearts"—as the fanzines had termed Fisher and Reynolds—were no more.

Taylor's mistake, however, was not sleeping with Fisher. It was failing to grovel before Hedda Hopper. Taylor had genuflected in the past; she knew the drill. But when Hopper rang to ask whether she planned to marry Fisher, Taylor had the temerity to suggest that Hopper was intrusive. So Hopper penalized Taylor, by publishing only a small part of what

Taylor had said: "Mike's dead and I'm alive." The quote was intended to turn fans against her, which it did.

Fisher bore the brunt of the anger. He lost his lucrative television gig hosting *Coke Time*. Reynolds, in contrast, got a huge career boost. She reinvented herself as the anti-Taylor: a devoted mother; a moral pillar, a *blonde*. In pigtails, without makeup, she held a press conference at her front door to discuss Fisher's betrayal. The cover of *Photoplay*'s January 1959 issue said it all: Reynolds, long-suffering, appears with her children, Carrie and Todd. The caption: "Can't daddy be with us all the time?"

Reynolds's antics made Taylor more defiant. To the chagrin of her mother, Sara, a Christian Scientist, and, for that matter, Fisher, a Jew, Elizabeth studied with Rabbi Max Nussbaum to convert to Reform Judaism, which in April 1959 she did.

In response to Taylor's embrace of Judaism, Reynolds flaunted her Christianity. In 1962, Reynolds published an advice book for girls called *If I Knew Then*. It contains some typical fare: how to be thin, popular, and keep a boy's mind off kissing. (This was not hard: she prescribes a "kitchen date" with actor Tab Hunter, who today is openly gay.) But the book also has a chapter on how and why girls should talk to Jesus. "Saying grace," she suggests, "is a wonderful way for a family to make a daily contact with God."

In 1959, as the Taylor-Reynolds skirmish heated up in Hollywood, producer Sam Spiegel miraculously appeared with a way out. He offered Taylor a lead in *Suddenly, Last Summer*, another Williams play, which he and screenwriter Gore Vidal would not allow to be gutted. He planned to shoot the film a long way from Los Angeles—in London, and on the coast of Spain. And he was brilliant at fending off the press. Shortly after shooting began, gossip columnist Louella Parsons published rumors of problems on the set of *Suddenly, Last Summer*—including an allegation that Taylor had become too fat for her part. Spiegel promptly fired off a telegram of rebuttal. It concluded: SORRY TO DISAPPOINT YOUR INFORMANT BUT NOBODY IS MAD AT ANYBODY AND IF ELIZABETH TAYLOR IS OVERWEIGHT I FOR ONE AM AT A LOSS TO SUGGEST WHAT THERE SHOULD BE LESS OF.

8

Suddenly, Last Summer, 1959

Insane is such a meaningless word. —Montgomery Clift as Dr. Cukrowicz to Elizabeth Taylor as Catherine Holly in *Suddenly, Last Summer*

Lobotomy is a very specific one. —Taylor, in reply

SUDDENLY, LAST SUMMER is lit with the stark black-and-white contrast of a monster movie or an episode of Rod Serling's original *Twilight Zone*. It opens in the women's ward of Lion's View, a falling-down Louisiana state mental hospital. The inmates—a kaleidoscope of catatonic husks, toothless babblers, and twitchy paranoiacs—inhabit a cylindrical tank called "the drum." The space is shadowy, menacing, and female viewers would do well to fear it. Lion's View has hired a new male surgeon. His specialty is the prefrontal lobotomy, an operation in which the right brain hemisphere is severed from the left. An operation that, before it fell out of favor in the 1960s, was overwhelmingly performed on women.

Tennessee Williams knew this operation well. In 1937—the year in which *Suddenly, Last Summer* is set—Williams's own sister, Rose, age twenty-eight, was lobotomized at the state asylum in Farmington, Missouri, where his mother, Edwina, had incarcerated her. Some Williams biographers believe that Williams's father, a violent drunk, had attempted to molest Rose, and the girl's accusations so upset Edwina that she gave Farmington permission to cut them out. (Or, more precisely, to pierce Rose's brain with an ice pick—the device preferred by many lobotomists, who drove it through the roof of a patient's eye socket, then tapped it with a hammer.)

Williams's sister was not the only famous victim. In 1941, Rosemary Kennedy, age twenty-three, sister of future U.S. president John F. Kennedy, was lobotomized at the request of her parents, Rose and Joseph P. Kennedy Sr. The girl had been disruptive—exhibiting mood swings (who, at twenty-three, doesn't?) and sneaking out of her convent school. The Kennedys hoped to excise her rebellion, which they did. The operation left her with infantile intelligence, urinary incontinence, and the inability to speak.

Neuropathologist Walter Freeman and his medical partner, neurosurgeon James Watts, were not stripped of their medical licenses for disabling Kennedy. They gained prestige. In 1949, Freeman nominated António Egas Moniz, the Portuguese doctor who invented the lobotomy, for a Nobel Prize—which, astonishingly, Moniz won. A year later, Freeman broke with Watts when Watts criticized Freeman's plan to streamline the procedure by substituting electric shock for traditional anesthesia. To demonstrate how well his new technique worked, Freeman barnstormed U.S. state hospitals in a van that came to be known as the "lobotomobile."

By 1959, however, when the film version of *Suddenly, Last Summer* came out, the press had exposed Kennedy's ordeal, as well as that of other victims. Audiences knew that a lobotomy was not, as one character suggests, "like having your tonsils out." But books such as Phyllis Chesler's 1972 landmark, *Women and Madness*, were still decades in the future. Drawing upon exhaustive research, Chesler documented how male mental health professionals have throughout history pathologized disruptive women. A woman who asserted herself sexually—or rebelled against her second-class societal role—was likely to be labeled crazy and locked up. (Or, in yet more primitive times, incinerated as a witch.)

Freeman was discredited in 1967, when he accidentally killed a woman on whom he was performing a *third* lobotomy. But psychotherapists continued to muzzle troublesome women, using antipsychotic drugs such as Thorazine (developed in the 1950s) instead of surgery.

Nor were psychiatrists unique in their insensitivity. Specialists in all fields, particularly gynecology, tended to ignore women's feelings. During the 1950s, male obstetricians used "twilight sleep" as an anesthetic for childbirth. The drug didn't ease a woman's agony; it just made her forget the pain afterward. Even today, some male doctors remain shockingly indifferent to women's welfare. This was evident in May 2010, when the American Academy of Pediatrics announced its willingness to serve the Muslim immigrant community by performing clitorectomies on girls. Happily, when blistering, immediate, and widespread criticism met the announcement, the AAP backpedaled.

In *Suddenly, Last Summer,* Elizabeth Taylor battles all the doctors who have ever used science against an inconvenient woman. She portrays Catherine Holly, a trauma victim, whose lost memories, if recovered, might destroy the reputation of her newly deceased cousin, Sebastian Venable. But because Williams created art, not agitprop, Catherine does not have a pat antagonist. Nothing in this movie is black-and-white, except its film stock. Doctors, Williams suggests, don't always practice medicine in a sterilized operating room; they work in the real world, with all its corruption. Sometimes, doctors can be tainted by this corruption. They can be manipulated by unscrupulous people—of whom there is no shortage in *Suddenly, Last Summer.*

Thanks to set designer Oliver Messel, Lion's View is an unmistakable snake pit. But compared with the New Orleans home of Catherine's aunt, Violet Venable, the state asylum is as cheery as a Disney theme park. Violet's overstuffed Victorian house surrounds a dank primeval garden, a tangle of clawlike shrubs and twisted tree-ferns, dripping with Spanish moss. A human skeleton adorns a wall niche. Carnivorous plants devour live flies. There, Violet obsesses on the flesh-eating birds that she and Sebastian, her son, witnessed while he was "looking for God" in the Galapagos.

As portrayed by Katharine Hepburn, Violet is over-the-top,

even for a pompous Garden District dowager with deep pockets. She enters her drawing room via a birdcage elevator: "The Emperor of Byzantium, when he received people in audience, would rise mysteriously in the air to the consternation of the visitors," she explains. "But as we are living in a democracy, I reverse the procedure. I don't rise; I come down."

Although Violet is a powerful woman, she is in no way a feminist. She recoils from the company of other women, with whom she feels she has nothing in common. She prefers to be around young men, such as her late son. "We were a famous couple," she tells Dr. Cukrowicz, the new surgeon at Lion's View, when he visits her. "People didn't speak of Sebastian and his mother or Mrs. Venable and her son, they said, 'Sebastian and Violet.'"

Cukrowicz doesn't raise an eyebrow. As portrayed by Montgomery Clift, he speaks with empathy. Yet his expressions are inscrutable. This may have been inadvertent—Clift's accident froze half his face. But it heightens his mystery; viewers can't quickly tell whether he's benign or not.

Cukrowicz's boss, who runs Lion's View, is not benign. He is an emblem of the coldhearted male medical establishment. Desperate to shore up his hospital, he places its needs above those of its individual patients. When Violet offers to donate a million dollars, he leaps, despite a large string attached to the gift. She demands that Cukrowicz lobotomize her niece, Catherine.

The girl, Violet explains, has been in a Catholic sanitarium since she returned from Spain last summer, where she had traveled with Sebastian. Delusional, she now "babbles" obscene things about Sebastian and how he died.

"I can't guarantee that a lobotomy would stop her—babbling," Cukrowicz tells Violet.

"But after the operation," Violet says with a twinkle, "who would believe her?"

Eager to impress the surgeon, Violet shows him Sebastian's art collection—sketches and paintings of erotic male nudes, including a toothsome Saint Sebastian penetrated by arrows. If Catherine's babbling includes allegations of sodomy, the viewer will not be surprised.

Cukrowicz next interviews Catherine, who is lucid and composed, to the annoyance of the nun who torments her by withholding cigarettes. After Cukrowicz offers to move Catherine to Lion's View, she adds to the picture he is forming of Sebastian: "'Famished for blondes. Tired of the dark ones.' That's the way he talked about people. As if they were items on a menu."

Catherine thrives at Lion's View. Alarmed by her niece's growing sanity, Violet offers Catherine's family money—if they can force her to undergo the lobotomy. Catherine bolts from them, accidentally fleeing to a more harrowing place: a catwalk above the men's section of the drum. When the male inmates see her, they lunge. Hooting, cawing, they clutch at her ankles. To me, this is the film's scariest scene. It foreshadows the revelation of cannibalism; the men, drooling, hunger for Catherine.

But it is also a metaphor for celebrity. Watching the scene, I understood how it must have felt to be Elizabeth

Taylor—above the mob but still not safe from it, unable to turn off her beauty when it attracted undesired strangers.

Tension mounts. Vexed by Cukrowicz's dawdling, his boss threatens to replace him with a compliant lobotomist. In a last-ditch effort to unearth the truth, Cukrowicz gathers Violet, his boss, and Catherine's family at Violet's home. In front of them, he injects Catherine with Sodium Pentothal and interrogates her.

As Catherine, Taylor commands the screen. Her words are incantatory, hypnotic. Her ordeal did not begin in Europe with Sebastian; she had been raped the previous winter. We see fragments of her horror—a montage of images, including the skeleton in Violet's garden and the final minutes of Sebastian's life. Then she blurts what Violet never wanted anyone to hear: for years, Sebastian had used Violet to procure men for him. But last summer, when Violet became too old, he recruited Catherine. Aghast, Catherine recalls the see-through bathing suit Sebastian made her wear in Spain: a magnet for rough youths—youths for purchase—some of whom later turned on him, ending his life and gouging hunks from his body.

In the face of this truth, Violet succumbs to madness. Catherine survives. That is her triumph. She stood up to authority. She blocked a misuse of power. She forced the male doctors—including Cukrowicz's boss—to think twice before lodging an ice pick in a sane woman's head.

* * *

Catherine's triumph is almost identical to that of the filmmakers: producer Sam Spiegel, director Joseph Mankiewicz, and screenwriter Gore Vidal. They stood up to authority. They blocked a misuse of power. They prevented the Production Code Administration and the Catholic Legion of Decency from completely eviscerating Williams's play.

This was hard to do. Much of the credit goes to Spiegel, whose first smart move was securing Vidal to adapt the play. Not only was Vidal a friend of Williams, or "the Bird," as he calls him; he was uniquely suited to address the concerns of the play's Roman Catholic critics. After the censors office flat-out nixed a synopsis of *Suddenly, Last Summer,* Vidal agreed to meet biweekly with a Roman Catholic priest during the writing process and show him drafts of the script.

Vidal doesn't recall which watchdog agency the priest represented: "They have so many of these torture groups—to try to keep literature and art out of commerce." But he remembers that the priest was not impressive: "He was one of the dumb ones, a Christian brother or something," which is to say: not a Jesuit or a canonical scholar. "And I knew so much more about the Catholic Church than he did."

This was not an idle boast. Vidal had exhaustively researched the early Christian Church for his 1962 novel, *Julian*, which deals with Julian Augustus, the fourth century pagan emperor who tried to stop the advance of Christianity in the Roman Empire. Emperor Julian terms Christians "Galileans," and he fears them. They will slaughter anyone who stands between them and political power.

In fairness to the intelligence of the priest, Vidal can be intimidating—even at age eighty-three and confined to a wheelchair, as he was when I interviewed him. When I arrived at his house, an assistant carried him downstairs. Regal in pajamas and a bathrobe, he greeted me by alluding to a line of Violet's from *Suddenly, Last Summer*—a line that he, not Williams, had written: "Because this is a democracy . . . I don't rise. I come down."

Vidal refused to turn the play into a moral fable about the evils of homosexuality. He did, however, construct the story so that his Catholic critics could read it as such if they chose to.

Cleverly, Vidal opens the film after Sebastian, the gay character, is dead—having expired in a horrific way that could be interpreted as "punishment" for his wickedness. In an uncensored movie, a handsome actor portraying Sebastian might have appeared in flashback scenes sipping daiquiris while Catherine flirted with attractive locals. In this film, Sebastian is a cipher, a faceless figure, who, in a flickering montage, meets a bad, if not entirely comprehensible, demise.

A few months after the film came out, when Vidal was stopped for speeding on New York's Taconic State Parkway, he learned just how baffling some viewers had found the ending. "The policeman recognized me and said, 'I just saw that movie you wrote. Was that guy a faggot?' " Vidal recalls. "I said, 'I think he was, yeah.' " And the policeman was exultant—because he had figured this out and his wife hadn't.

Some of the film's murkiness, however, was not in the script but in the direction. Under the spell of Swedish auteur

Ingmar Bergman (one of whose characters famously plays chess with Death), Joseph L. Mankiewicz peppered *Suddenly, Last Summer* with enigmatic symbols. After viewing the climactic montage, Spiegel began calling him "Ingmar Mankiewicz."

In the fall of 1959, Spiegel submitted a finished version of the film to the Production Code Administration Appeals Board. "The story admittedly deals with an [*sic*] homosexual, but one who pays for his sin with his life," Spiegel argued. And "there should be no offense on religious grounds because the mother and son are obviously psychopaths."

Things had changed at the Production Code Administration since Stevens's scuffle over *A Place in the Sun*. In 1954, Joseph Breen retired as chief enforcer. He was replaced by Geoffrey Shurlock, his former assistant. Unlike Breen, who had kept apart from Hollywood, Shurlock seemed to enjoy Spiegel's company. On November 16, 1959, Shurlock wrote to Spiegel: "I don't need to tell you what a treat it is for us to meet you under all circumstances, and even in the melee of an appeals hearing." Shurlock also enjoyed what appears to have been a bribe: "I must thank you again for getting me in to that magnificent performance of 'Figaro' at the Metropolitan."

Whether by dint of persuasion or payoff, Spiegel prevailed at the hearing. Both the Production Code Administration and the Legion of Decency approved the film. Unfortunately, the critics did not. In an emblematic review, *Variety* called it "the most bizarre film ever made by any major American company."

At first, Vidal recalls, Spiegel was "furious about how terrible the reviews were and he blamed me. He said, 'You ruined it, you ruined it.' I said, 'I have not. Those reviews will make it the most successful movie of your career, even more than the dreadful *Bridge on the River Kwai.*'" And as is so often the case, Vidal was right.

Columbia's cunning publicity campaign also helped. Its ads managed to be both smug and titillating. They showed Taylor in that notorious see-through swimsuit with the caption: "Cathy knew she was being used for evil." In this context, of course, "evil" meant "procuring." When you view the film today, however, only one true evil leaps out: the willingness of some male doctors to maim a healthy woman for money.

When *Suddenly, Last Summer* wrapped, Taylor still owed MGM one last movie. She fought to be released from her contract, but the studio fought harder. She had to accept the film it imposed: *BUtterfield 8*. Seething with resentment—and determined to slow the production—Taylor struggled against the role of Gloria Wandrous. At some point, however, she stopped resisting. She embraced Gloria, making her bigger and more memorable than the small-minded plot in which both Gloria—and Taylor—were stuck. She made Gloria what in the 1980s would be termed a "sex-positive" feminist.

9

BUtterfield 8, 1960

Now I get it—you pick the man. He doesn't pick you. —Laurence Harvey as Weston Liggett to Elizabeth Taylor as Gloria Wandrous in *BUtterfield 8.* (Liggett made this observation after Wandrous plunged her stiletto heel into his instep.)

There should be developed in this story an attitude of compassion for Gloria, not one of glorification. The story should seem to indicate that she might have been a great woman if it were not for the fact that she was a sick one. —E. G. Dougherty, Production Code Administration memo, October 16, 1959

POOR GLORIA WANDROUS. She was born—or invented—before society was ready for her. Gloria is the central character in *BUtterfield 8*, John O'Hara's 1935 novel, as well as Daniel Mann's 1960 movie of the same name.

Gloria may be Elizabeth Taylor's most magnificent character, as well as her most feminist. But to appreciate Gloria, one must view her through the lens of today. On a contemporary university campus, Gloria would be an archetypal coed. But in 1935—and even in 1960—she was an object of scorn. Gloria is in touch with her sexual feelings and chooses to satisfy them, as do "nice" girls in today's culture of "hook-ups," liaisons that don't necessarily lead to marriage. Young women who "hook up" don't view this as an alternative to marriage; most still seek that institution's prestige and tax advantages. But they wisely realize that not all attractions last forever. In the twenty-first century, Gloria's behavior seems both prudent and clear-eyed. But in 1959, the Production Code Administration called it "nymphomaniac."

In her essay "Lusting for Freedom," feminist Rebecca Walker emphasizes the value of sexual experimentation to the emotional health of young women—as a stepping stone to forging enduring relationships. Almost more important than the sex itself is the permission to engage in it. Walker disparages "sex where our agency is denied"—sex divorced from female desire—and the institutions that condemn women for pursuing pleasure. "For giving bodies what they want and crave, for exploring ourselves and others, we are punished like Eve reaching for more knowledge," she writes. "We are called sluts and whores. We are considered impure and psychotic."

The term "pro-sex feminist" arose during the early 1980s, when some feminists aligned with social conservatives to fight pornography. In this debate, the feminists who championed the First Amendment—and dared to consider pleasure a woman's right—were called "pro-sex" or "sex-positive." Writer Ellen Willis explains: "Confronted with a right-wing backlash bent on reversing social acceptance of non-marital, non-procreative sex, feminists like me, who saw sexual liberalism as deeply flawed by sexism but nonetheless a source of crucial gains for women, found themselves at odds with feminists who dismissed the sexual revolution as monolithically sexist and shared many of the attitudes of conservative moralists." Gloria would likely have shared Willis's views.

At the beginning of *BUtterfield 8*, Gloria wakes up alone, in the rumpled bed of Weston Liggett, portrayed by Laurence Harvey, a man she met mere hours earlier. The camera zooms in on her left hand, conspicuously unencumbered by a wedding ring. Gloria is a tiny bit hungover, which is also something young women today are permitted to be. The Production Code Administration, however, referred to occasional overindulgences by women as "alcoholic." (Spencer Tracy's character in *Father of the Bride* routinely drank until he passed out, but the Production Code folk never branded him with the A-word.)

The movie version of *BUtterfield 8* divides into two clear sections: an opening movement based on O'Hara's book, and a closing movement shaped by the Production Code Administration. In section one, Gloria is a beacon of female sexuality and power. She boldly defies marital convention and rejects men who repel her, no matter how much money they offer. She will not be rented like a prostitute or owned like a chattel—or like a wife, for that matter. In the fancy Manhattan apartment of Liggett, who is married to another woman, Gloria finds a note that says, "$250.00. Enough?" And assuming that the money is for her, not for the dress that he ripped, she declares her independence, scrawling "No Sale" in lipstick on an ornate mirror.

Equally memorable, in a later scene, Gloria makes clear to

Liggett that she desires *him*, not his wallet. "Put your assets away," she scoffs. "You couldn't match what I've already turned down." When he interprets this as a negotiating ploy, she impales his foot with her spike heel—an image of such startling female strength that I gasped when I first saw it. The scene was recorded in one long shot. Harvey's fluid face captures Liggett's confusion. He is at first aroused, then aghast. If Gloria picks partners based on her own desire, he wonders, does she then drop them when she pleases? "Without a parachute," she smirks.

Gloria is quick-witted and verbal. After swimming to consciousness in Liggett's bedroom—then borrowing his wife's mink coat because Liggett had destroyed her dress—she heads to the Greenwich Village apartment of her childhood buddy, Steve, lamely portrayed by Eddie Fisher. "Sunday morning and Scotch on your breath?" Steve says. "Well, it's good Scotch," Gloria rejoins.

Out of respect for her mother, with whom she lives, Gloria refuses to return home naked under an expensive fur. Her mother works hard to ignore Gloria's idiosyncrasies, but this might be too much to overlook. She asks Steve for help. "I'm all she has," Gloria tells him, referring to her mother. "So we have to lie to each other."

Reluctantly, Steve's girlfriend, Norma, lends Gloria a suit, snidely remarking that it "shocks easily." Norma is a tedious, self-righteous blonde—Debbie Reynolds without the talent. Of course Gloria gets the better of Norma in their exchange. But the problem is, Gloria permits Norma to frame the conversation with her bourgeois notions of morality.

Had Gloria come of age in the 1990s, she might have critiqued those notions, as well as the lack of self-consciousness with which Norma embraces them.

In part one of *BUtterfield 8*, Gloria is so out-of-step with society that she seems like a time traveler from the future—a visitor from the 1980s or early '90s, when academic theories of gender explored the social construction of heterosexuality. During these years, a new discipline—queer studies—emerged at universities. This discipline looked at groups that had been marginalized by their sexuality: gay men, lesbians, bisexuals, and transgendered people. It embraced prostitutes as "sex workers," who exposed the tacit economic transactions of heterosexuality. Before this line of thinking, even a suffragist like Rebecca West (1882–1983), who defined "feminist" as an antonym of "doormat" and defiantly bore an out-of-wedlock child, was dismissive of female sex workers. West resisted looking at the ways in which their transactions with straight men might be more honest than the identical but veiled transactions within a heterosexual marriage.

I can imagine a latter-day Gloria contributing to an anthology such as Jill Nagle's *Whores and Other Feminists*, a groundbreaking 1994 collection of scholarship from the intersection of queer studies and feminism. I envision Gloria defiant, explaining to Norma that what Norma calls "moral" is simply the oppressive "norm of white procreative heterosexuality."

I picture Gloria using words like those of contributor Eva Pendleton, a professional prostitute who at the time of publication was earning a Ph.D. in American studies at New York University: "Heterosexuality as a social system depends upon the specter of unchastity in order to constitute itself. The 'good wife' as a social category cannot exist without the 'whore' . . . Each of these othered positions exists to reinforce the norm of white procreative heterosexuality."

Norma's priggishness, Gloria might also have added, probably has less to do with principles than with paranoia about social class. As filmmaker and pornography scholar Laura Kipnis wrote, notions of "propriety" and "bad taste" arose during the ascendancy of the bourgeoisie, which codified rigid rules as a way to "separate themselves from the noisy lower orders." Because their social positions are inherited, aristocrats can be indifferent to such rules. And Bohemians define themselves in contrast to the rules, *pour épater la bourgeoisie*, as the saying goes.

In *BUtterfield 8*, although Steve means well, he is too dim and conformist to be a useful friend to Gloria. He clings to a galling 1950s misconception: parents who deviate from traditional gender roles will inevitably warp their kids. Steve explains this to Norma: when Gloria was a little girl, her father died and her mother went to work—so of course Gloria turned out badly. Such propaganda dominated mid-twentieth-century pop culture, reaching its apotheosis in *Rebel Without a Cause*, when James Dean's character has no choice but to fall in with a delinquent crowd. He once saw his dad wearing an apron.

Gloria did, in fact, suffer as a teenager, but not because her mother worked. When Mrs. Wandrous tried to return to a traditional housewife role, the man to whom she was engaged molested Gloria. Gloria enjoyed the sensations but felt sullied by them—a conflict common to abuse victims and one that psychotherapists often successfully treat. Gloria's Freudian analyst, however, never addressed Gloria's problems, but this wasn't entirely his fault. The Production Code forbade him from improving her mental health. For *BUtterfield 8* to obtain its seal of approval, Gloria had to be portrayed as "sick," E. G. Dougherty, a Code official, told Pandro S. Berman, the film's producer.

The revelation of abuse opens the film's unfortunate second section. Abruptly, Gloria becomes infected by patriarchy—or, in the vernacular of the 1950s, "respectability." She begins second-guessing everything that is clean and noble and strong inside her. She starts saying things like, "By some miracle, I'm like everybody else. I'm in love." Mann must have found this line as comical as I did. When she says it, he frames her head with a plate on the wall, so that she appears to have a halo.

"I was the slut of all time," she blurts to her mother, who slaps her—which I myself would have done, though for a different reason: words like "whore" and "slut" are merely the flip side of "good wife." They imply that a woman cannot own her own body. She exists only in relationship to men.

Liggett does not love his wife. But thanks to the Production Code Office, he has sanctimonious friends who try to make him feel bad about this. "You married a lovely woman and you blame her for the life you lead," one tells him. On the other hand, because Liggett's wife, Emily, refuses to live in the same city with him, even the censors realized that she might have had a hand in their estrangement. In August 1959, before filming began, E. G. Dougherty demanded that Emily be "re-written so as to eliminate what now appears to be a social, if not moral, justification for Liggett to look elsewhere for his love life."

No amount of revision could make Geoffrey Shurlock like the script. "Liggett appears to have no recognition whatever of the immorality of his adultery, and its relationship to his marriage," he grumbled. In the novel, this is, of course, the point. Liggett has not enjoyed sex with his wife since *before* they were married. Soon after the wedding, Emily's closest childhood friend seduced him. "From that moment on," O'Hara writes, "he never loved Emily again." This occurred long before he met Gloria.

O'Hara's novel is less a character study than a mural—a seamy, sprawling portrait of New York City during the Great Depression. None of his characters represents good or evil; they are just flawed people muddling through an imperfect world. The Gloria that he created was not an avatar of sex-positive feminism; she was a victim of her economic circumstances. Taylor brought a modern sensibility to Gloria, making her more compelling—and seemingly self-aware—than she was originally drawn.

Once Gloria succumbs to conventionality, the vital, animated woman in part one ceases to exist. She might as well be dead; and soon she actually is. In the novel, while fleeing from Liggett, she falls (or jumps) from a steamer bound for Boston. In the film, she crashes her convertible.

Taylor did not want to play Gloria—because of Gloria's bad-girl behavior, she told the press. And at least one person believed her. "MGM must have thought the image was perfect—Elizabeth Taylor as a whore and homewrecker," Fisher wrote in his memoir "They wouldn't let her work on *Cleopatra* or anything else until she made the picture."

Therein, of course, lies her real motivation. Taylor's standard fee from MGM was $125,000 per movie. Producer Walter Wanger offered her $1 million to portray Cleopatra. "The trouble had nothing to do with the fact that Gloria was a call girl," Pandro S. Berman told Brenda Maddox. Taylor simply wanted more money.

Unable to break the contract, Taylor lobbied without success for a stronger script. The screenplay's flaws, however, were not literary but ideological. O'Hara's novel had critiqued the society that destroyed Gloria. But Dougherty and Shurlock, who had final say over the movie, viewed Gloria's rebellion as the problem and punishment as the solution.

After viewing the finished picture, Fisher called it "trash," which was certainly true of his part in it. In a charitable appraisal, the *Saturday Review* called Fisher "a non-actor, much as certain successful books have been called non-books." The *Harvard Lampoon* named him Worst Actor of the Year.

Taylor never forgave MGM for delaying her work on *Cleopatra*. She expressed her anger at the studio after seeing a rough cut of *BUtterfield 8*. Before arriving at MGM to watch it, she and Fisher dined at Trader Vic's, a Beverly Hills restaurant known for its potent cocktails. The couple brought two big cups of Scorpions—a blend of rum, brandy, and citrus juices—to sip during the screening. When the lights came up afterward, Taylor hurled her drink at the screen. Then she lurched to the office of Sol Siegel, MGM's head of production, and scrawled "No Sale!" in lipstick on his door. Moviegoers, however, did not share her opinion. *BUtterfield 8* became a sensation, earning Taylor both $15 million and her first Academy Award.

For no reason besides coincidence, 1960 was a big year for prostitutes in the movies. *Never on Sunday* (a Greek film set in Piraeus) and *The World of Suzie Wong* (an English film set in Hong Kong) also explored the theme. The Production Code Administration had no authority over foreign films, which was fortunate because Shurlock hated these two. In a letter defending *BUtterfield 8* as a "moral story," he railed against the idea of prostitution being treated "sentimentally," as in *Suzie Wong* or, worse, "gaily," as in *Never on Sunday.*

In *BUtterfield 8*, thanks to the hard work of his office, "sin" looks "exactly the way it should, repulsive and degrading." And Gloria gets what a sinner deserves: "The girl is conscious of her wrongdoing, bemoans her weakness, berates herself to her mother and to her young musician boy friend; and, at the end, in an attempt to flee from falling back into evil, she has an accident and is killed."

Had Shurlock stopped there, his letter would have exposed him as a bully and a prig. But he continued, revealing himself as an ignoramus.

"In the last century, issues between good and evil were much more clearly drawn," he wrote, citing Gustave Flaubert's *Madame Bovary* and Leo Tolstoy's *Anna Karenina* as examples of moral tales. "In both these novels, the adulteresses died horribly," he noted, pleased that they met an appropriate fate. He then suggested that Flaubert and Tolstoy "would have been scandalized at the treatment of prostitution in *Never on Sunday.*"

Shurlock's interpretation is, of course, exactly the opposite of what the authors intended. Both Flaubert and Tolstoy were sympathetic to their women characters. Their goal was to criticize the bourgeois social conventions that destroyed two healthy, lively, women. Nor would either author have been "scandalized" by *Never on Sunday.* Though they might have gagged at the ending of *BUtterfield 8.* "I love prostitution," Flaubert famously said, "and for itself, too, quite apart from what is beneath." (This line is also often translated "quite apart from its carnal aspects.") Tolstoy was also a lifelong fan, despite the venereal disease he contracted in his youth.

After watching *BUtterfield 8* many times, I can barely recall its final scenes. "The ending," *New York Times* critic Bosley Crowther wrote, "is absurd." But I will never forget "No Sale!" scribbled in lipstick or the spike heel grinding into Liggett's shoe. Taylor breathed life into the defiant Gloria, burning her into our collective memory. Then she sleepwalked through the moralistic *mishegoss* imposed by the Production Code.

Taylor couldn't rescue Gloria from the censors. But at least she minimized their damage.

10

1960–1962

IN *SUDDENLY, LAST SUMMER*, Elizabeth Taylor gave form and believability to Catherine Holly, a brave trauma victim who stands up to the male medical establishment. In real life, however, actors can be different from the characters they play. Taylor suffered from health problems going back to her adolescence. And perhaps because her mother was a Christian Scientist, for whom medical treatment is anathema, Taylor herself became an ardent consumer of the healing arts.

On the set of *Giant*, she often spent her off-camera time in a wheelchair, tormented by sciatica and numbness in her legs. Her chronic back problems had begun in childhood. While learning to jump horses for *National Velvet*, she took a variety of spills that caused injuries. But her shooting schedule didn't permit adequate leisure for them to heal. In 1957, after accidentally tumbling down some stairs, she underwent a four-hour surgery at New York's Harkness Pavilion to fuse the crushed disks in her spine. Her then-consort Mike Todd did his best to make her stay pleasurable. He installed himself in the room next door and purchased a Renoir, a Pissarro, a Monet, and a Frans Hals to liven up her joyless hospital walls. So blissful, in fact, was her doctor-ordered sojourn that within the year—and not long after delivering her daughter, Liza, by cesarean section—Taylor arranged for an unnecessary appendectomy. This time she booked Todd into the adjoining suite and forbade him to leave until she had recovered.

In his memoir, Eddie Fisher writes with odd wistfulness of his time with Taylor and its glamorous backdrops: a bungalow at the Beverly Hills Hotel, a suite at the Park Lane in Manhattan, quarters designed by Oliver Messel at the Dorchester in London—as well as emergency rooms on two continents. As I read his descriptions, I began to understand. When I needed a break from this manuscript, I stayed at a hotel. But when you live in a hotel, where do you go to escape? To the hospital.

This is only half-facetious. As a child, Taylor supported her parents financially. After Todd's death, she supported her children—by herself. To survive, her family depended on her; and to support them, Taylor depended on her appearance. She couldn't look puffy or haggard on screen. She had to look fantastic—or in any event, thin. If her director told her to smile, she had to radiate sunshine. She had to dredge within herself to play a scene with feeling. She was always going, going, going. But if she became really sick—sick enough to die—the carousel stopped. A dead star could derail a film and cost a studio money. In sickness, she could escape her burdens. In sickness, she could rest.

Fisher recounts one harrowing near-death experience after another. While shooting *BUtterfield 8*, Taylor fell prey to pneumonia and could barely breathe. Passed out from cold medication, she was whisked on a stretcher from the Park Lane to Harkness Pavilion. As the ambulance approached the emergency room, however, Fisher recalls, Taylor sat up, rummaged for a compact, and handed Fisher her purse. "Get me my lip gloss," she ordered.

As soon as Taylor recovered from pneumonia, she again went to a hospital—this time as a visitor to Fisher's ailing mother in Philadelphia. But the pull of the ER proved irresistible. Before returning to New York, Taylor slipped on some ice, sprained her ankle, and received emergency treatment. She left Philadelphia on crutches.

After many illness-related delays, *BUtterfield 8* finally wrapped. In September 1960, Taylor and Fisher settled in London, where *Cleopatra* was to be filmed. England was good for Taylor's financial health. For tax reasons, she had demanded that the movie be shot there. But the damp air was bad for her lungs. Almost as soon as she moved into the Dorchester she got sick.

Taylor was not popular in London. Tabloids continued to blame her for Fisher's divorce. Worse, she offended the British hairdresser's union, which staged a strike on the set of *Cleopatra.* She had demanded that Sidney Guilaroff, her MGM stylist, be permitted to arrange her hair for the movie. The Brits were furious. What was so special about her hair that they couldn't comb it?

Nor, as Rouben Mamoulian, *Cleopatra*'s director, discovered, was London in winter a plausible substitute for Alexandria, Egypt, at any time of the year. Wanger had palm trees flown in from Hollywood to make Pinewood Studios resemble Egypt's Mediterranean coast, but he could do nothing about the bitter cold and fog. Peter Finch, who had been cast as Julius Caesar, and Stephen Boyd, who had been cast as Mark Antony, shivered beneath their metal breastplates. Taylor coughed and wheezed in her hotel room. In January 1961, after a row with 20th Century Fox over the script, Mamoulian resigned. In February, Joseph Mankiewicz took over as director. He tried to interest Laurence Durrell and Lillian Hellman in working on the screenplay. When they declined, Mankiewicz began writing it himself.

Taylor's health worsened. The problems, Fisher explained, had as much to do with her back as with her lungs. She needed shots of Demerol, which he administered, to ease the chronic pain. By late February, fighting staphylococcus pneumonia, she burned constantly with fever. At night she slept beneath an oxygen tent in her hotel room. On March 3, 1961, the infection and painkillers became too much. She slipped into a coma.

Fisher noticed nothing unusual. But Taylor's private nurse flew into action, summoning a doctor, who began mouth-to-mouth resuscitation. Lashed to a stretcher, Taylor was rushed to the London Clinic, where Fisher, in shock, gave permission for doctors to plunge a knife into his wife's throat. The incision created a "tracheotomy," a passage through which air could again reach Taylor's congested lungs.

With a tube poking through a hole in her neck, Taylor was alive but just barely. She still couldn't kick the infection. The crowds that had railed against her—for stealing

Reynolds's husband, for snubbing the British hairdressers—suddenly rallied in support. "Hundreds of people kept vigil day and night while Elizabeth fought for her life," Fisher wrote. "People everywhere loved her and were praying for her recovery."

Visitors like Tennessee Williams, John Wayne, and Truman Capote struggled to cheer her. Cards and letters poured in—so many that the hospital collected them in laundry baskets. Wanger recalls a telegram sent from the United States: SIX THOUSAND OF US ARE PRAYING FOR YOU AT THE BOEING PLANT. WE KNOW YOU'LL PULL THROUGH. But the stubborn infection would not capitulate. As Fisher tells it, a week after the tracheotomy, a British doctor injected Taylor with gamma globulin. And the infection finally gave up.

Discharged from the hospital, Taylor identified with Lazarus. She flew to Los Angeles, where she described her ordeal at a fund-raiser for Cedars of Lebanon and Mount Sinai hospitals. "Dying, as I remember it, is many things," she said. Mostly, it was lonely, and she was glad to be back. But she remained in touch with the angel of death, whom she met on the other side, and who often told her—psychically—when other people would die.

Nominated for Best Actress in *BUtterfield 8*, Taylor planned to attend the Academy Awards ceremony. Her main competitor was Shirley MacLaine, nominated for *The Apartment*. Today MacLaine is as well known for her psychic experiences as for her acting. A believer in reincarnation, she has written ten books that detail her past lives. In 1961, however, MacLaine was the rationalist and Taylor the mystic. And one wonders whether Taylor's win—the triumph of the mystic—might have inspired MacLaine's spiritual journey. Before Taylor returned from the grave, MacLaine was the odds-on favorite. Without rancor, MacLaine said, "I lost to a tracheotomy."

Fortified by her Oscar win, as well as a summer in Los Angeles, Taylor and Fisher flew to Rome where she began the final version of *Cleopatra.* While Taylor had languished in the hospital, version one had officially bitten the dust. In the new iteration, Rex Harrison was Julius Caesar, and Richard Burton was Mark Antony,

Taylor and Burton were not immediately drawn to each other. Acclaimed as a Shakespearean actor, Burton dismissed Taylor as "MGM's Little Miss Mammary." As he watched her work, however, he came to admire her craft. From the get-go, he had coveted Taylor's earning power. Soon he would come to covet Taylor herself.

Walter Wanger recalls their first scene together—in Cleopatra's Roman villa—on January 22, 1962. Taylor was "elegant in a simple yellow silk gown." Burton was "handsome, arrogant, and vigorous" in his knee-length toga. And between the two of them, "you could almost feel the electricity." By mid-February, the Burton-Taylor love affair had exploded, ripping their respective marriages asunder. The press called it *Le Scandale. L'Osservatore della Domenica*, the Vatican weekly, called it "erotic vagrancy." Vatican Radio called it "the caprices of adult children." And the publicity department at 20th Century Fox called it a godsend.

Typically, the Vatican did not comment on the private lives of movie stars. But Taylor had galled the papacy to its core. Not because of her extramarital affair; that was commonplace, slight. But because of something else—something truly extraordinary—something no undeserving erotic vagrant should have been permitted to accomplish. In London one year earlier, Taylor had died. But she had not stayed that way. She had—to the Vatican's horror—been resurrected.

11

Cleopatra, 1963

Alexandria had its share of female mathematicians, doctors, painters, and poets. This did not mean such women were above suspicion. As always, an educated woman was a dangerous woman. —Stacy Schiff, *Cleopatra: A Life*, 2010

First I shall want something to eat. —Elizabeth Taylor as Cleopatra preparing for her suicide

CLEOPATRA IS NEITHER a great movie nor a feminist one. But it had the potential to be both. Two seeming sure-bets were going for it. The first was the historical Queen Cleopatra VII of Egypt: a cunning politician and accomplished scholar who built a legendary library and spoke eight languages. She was not a fool for love. To obtain her throne, she murdered her brothers. To hold on to it, she conducted love affairs with her enemies—or, in any event, rulers of the empire that most threatened hers: Rome. Her first Roman lover was Julius Caesar; her second, Mark Antony. These were not romances. They were tactical alliances, sealed, in the case of Caesar, with a son, Caesarion.

The second attribute was Elizabeth Taylor. As Leslie Benedict in *Giant*, Taylor had projected brains, backbone, and a brilliance at behind-the-scenes manipulation—qualities no absolute ruler should be without. But this wasn't why producer Walter Wanger agreed to pay her $1 million. He needed her to do something only she could do: override the audience's prefrontal cortex, as she had in *A Place in the Sun*. He needed her to electrify viewers with primitive feeling. He needed her to whisper the Greek or Latin or Egyptian equivalent of "Tell Mama. Tell Mama all."

Taylor was also a real-life star, determined to display the traits that pop culture demanded of its luminaries. Just as ancient Egyptians needed their rulers to be divine—Cleopatra declared herself an incarnation of the goddess Isis—so, too, midcentury fans required stars to be moody, unreliable, and petulant. During the making of *Cleopatra*, Taylor worked hard to satisfy them. Not all directors and producers, however, valued such dedication to the harsh dictates of stardom. Some grew cross when stars went AWOL, nursing hangovers or sniffles. When, for example, Marilyn Monroe was shooting *Something's Got to Give*, a costly project that vied with *Cleopatra* for 20th Century Fox's dwindling resources, director George Cukor fired Monroe . . . for behaving like a movie star.

Wanger, though, understood stardom and its crushing pressure to appear capricious. He deflected Taylor's critics with a quote from director Billy Wilder: "I have a healthy aunt in Vienna who would come on set on time, know her lines, and always be ready. But no one would pay to see her at the box office."

Wanger also grasped extreme emotions. He himself had served time for a crime of passion: shooting the purported lover of his then-wife, actress Joan Bennett. Wanger hoped to deliver both Cleopatra's ice and Taylor's fire—to make the Egyptian queen as vivid as Barbara Graham, the ex-junkie death-row inmate in Wanger's searing 1958 movie, *I Want to Live!* Critics had loved that movie, even critics who supported capital punishment, which the film condemned. Portraying Graham, actress Susan Hayward won an Oscar.

But Wanger's dreams for *Cleopatra* never panned out. Perhaps they were too big for his time, the 1950s, when conformity, McCarthyism, and disbelief in the full humanity of women kept people and ideas small. But you can't say Wanger didn't try. Taylor tried, too. As did Joseph Mankiewicz, *Cleopatra*'s director, and 20th Century Fox, the studio that it pushed toward bankruptcy. Even the studio heads tried: Spyros Skouras, who initiated the project, and his successor, Darryl Zanuck, who ripped the movie away from Mankiewicz and hacked out scenes essential to its exposition. (After completing a cut that ran about six hours, Mankiewicz begged Zanuck to release the film in two parts; Zanuck refused.)

Cleopatra differs from most movies in this book—films whose nimble passages outnumber those that fall flat. The movie occasionally catches fire, but it quickly dies out. Mark Antony's stark assessment of himself could also apply to many people who worked on the film: "Meaning to do the best, I suppose I could not have done worse."

Imperfection, however, is why one must study *Cleopatra*. It teaches us not about 48 to 31 B.C. but about A.D. 1958 to 1963. Historical dramas often say more about the times in which they were made than the era in which they are set. Likewise, the characters in such dramas reflect the world of their writers. For example, in both *Julius Caesar* and *Antony and Cleopatra*, Shakespeare imagined an Egyptian woman who was tougher and wiser than both of her Roman consorts. He saw Cleopatra thorough the lens of the sixteenth century, when a formidable woman, Queen Elizabeth I, occupied the English throne.

Dramatists in the 1950s, however, had no Queen Bess to inspire them. Before 1969, when Golda Meir became prime minister of Israel, and 1979, when Margaret Thatcher assumed the same post in the United Kingdom, women did not hold visible power in the West. During the years when *Cleopatra* moved from page to screen, feminist thinker Betty Friedan, then a suburban New York housewife, struggled to discern why so few women rose to the top of governments, corporations, or, for that matter, their professions. She detailed her findings in *The Feminine Mystique*, an angry book that came out the same year as *Cleopatra* and became an instant bestseller.

After World War II, Friedan noticed, more "women than ever before were going to college—but fewer of them were going on from college to become physicians, philosophers, poets, doctors, lawyers, stateswomen, social pioneers, even college professors." Women would strive to reach a certain level, then—seemingly of their own volition—withdraw from the ascent. They had bought into a curious postwar ethos: because of their gender, they existed not to fulfill their potential but to fulfill the potential of others. Their role was not to live, but to live through—gaining satisfaction exclusively by way of their husbands and children.

Friedan called this pattern "the forfeited self." She blamed it on "the feminine mystique," a cult of female self-abnegation that maintained its grip through fear. The mystique impelled women to cower before the bogeyman of unfemininity—a scourge alleged to render them repulsive to men. Although *Cleopatra* was supposed to have been about the most powerful woman in the ancient world—an autocrat who seduced men with her wit and not her looks—the film fell prey to its time. Taylor could not do that much to project Cleopatra's independence and strength. The part had been written to show her clinginess and frailty.

The film cites Plutarch, Suetonius, and Appian as its sources—the same Roman historians whom Shakespeare likely read. But it also credits Carlo Maria Franzero's *The Life and Times of Cleopatra*, a 1950s middle-brow biography that was also a paean to the feminine mystique. In his book, Franzero recognizes Cleopatra's intelligence: "How soon, how soon Cleopatra must have seen through the bombast of Mark Antony, who could not conquer Persia with all the treasure of Egypt she had put at his disposal, and who abandoned the decision at Actium to chase after her in a mad fit of passion."

But Franzero never lets Cleopatra's intelligence prevail.

He always eclipses it with "that touch of frailty that is part of the enchantment of femininity that stirs the emotions and imaginations of great men."

Franzero's viewpoint informs the movie. Like the coeds in Friedan's book, the adolescent Cleopatra strives to become educated. As a young woman, she doesn't live through her male relatives; she murders them. But also like the women in Friedan's book, she is transformed by marriage and motherhood. Not tamed, exactly. Franzero's Cleopatra still itches to control the world. But only so that she can give it to her Roman lover and her eldest son.

The real-life Cleopatra was not Egyptian but Greek, descended from Ptolemy, a general under Alexander the Great who founded the dynasty that controlled Egypt from 323 to 30 B.C. Because she was a Ptolemy, transferring power to her son would not be an act of a doting mother or one of self-annihilation. It was the same tactical necessity that compelled every monarch before and after her to produce an heir: riding on her son's future was the future of the royal line.

But no historical reason exists to portray her as a slave to her emotions. "I will not have love as my master!" Taylor's Cleopatra hisses at Antony, whom she bedded with seeming cold-bloodedness to solidify a strategic alliance. Yet when Antony, also for tactical reasons, marries the sister of his Roman archrival, Octavian, she carries on like a jilted teenager, rather than the shrewd politician that she is.

Near the end of the movie, when she must choose between her man and her empire, she abandons all pretense of reason: "Without you, Antony, this is not a world I want to live in, much less conquer."

Cleopatra's problems with narration and structure, however, stem from more than the feminine mystique. The film was made during a painful upheaval in the movie business. By 1960, the studio system was on its last legs. Yet it had to marshal its remaining strength to contend with an unforeseen competitor: television.

In the 1950s, television blindsided the movie industry—stealing its audience and threatening its primacy. Television was free and easily consumed. And shows like *Playhouse 90* established it as a medium for intimate, idea-driven drama. To pry viewers out of their homes, movies had to offer what the small screen couldn't: spectacle—splashy, Technicolor pageants.

Typically, telling a story and creating a spectacle are antithetical challenges. Story gains power from nuance, from getting deep inside the characters' heads. Spectacle gains power from eye-popping effects, from actions that swirl around the characters.

Mankiewicz was a first-rate storyteller. In such classics as *All About Eve*, he created complex women characters whose clashes riveted audiences. In *Suddenly, Last Summer*, he coaxed a strong performance from Taylor. But for *Cleopatra*, this was not enough.

Life magazine's 1961 feature on the making of *Cleopatra*

reveals the lengths to which movies would go to upstage television. The piece fixates on color and spectacle: the "army of 4,000 being drilled to fight mighty land battles," the 1,500 ships "for naval engagements," the insane vibrancy of Cleopatra's costumes. (Taylor sports a brassy funereal headdress on the magazine's cover.) The article doesn't mention television, but it doesn't have to. Ads for the rival medium filled the magazine: Philco's "Cool-Chassis," Admiral's "Automatic Picture Contrast Restoration," Motorola's "Golden Tube Sentry Unit."

In principle, story and spectacle should be able to coexist in a film. But few directors balance them successfully. In *Gone with the Wind*, director Victor Fleming mixed the two, moving back and forth between an intimate love story and a sweeping mural. The contrast captured the magnitude of war: its vast fields of devastation; its tiny shattered lives.

Under different circumstances, Mankiewicz might have realized similar results with *Cleopatra*. But when he replaced Rouben Mamoulian as its director, the film was already over budget and behind schedule. Plus it had no script. Many people had been paid to write one—Sidney Buchman, Ranald MacDougall, Ben Hecht, among them. But no one could make it work. Mankiewicz had to write the script himself—on an insane deadline—while he directed the movie.

To do this, he filmed by day and wrote by night, battling exhaustion with amphetamine shots. If fatigue dulled his eye for nuance, this served him well. He couldn't afford to fuss over subtleties. He had to command a navy. He had to bark orders via an interpreter at four thousand Italian extras pretending to be Roman soldiers. He couldn't even be Cecil B. DeMille; he had to be General George S. Patton.

Not surprisingly, his characters sometimes took a backseat to their lavish world. Cleopatra's grand entrance into Rome, for example, should have exposed her firestorm of conflicting emotions. She had reasons to feel triumphant: she controlled Egypt's bounty and was the mother of Julius Caesar's only son. But she also had grounds for fear: Ceasar was legally married to someone else, and the Roman senate was already plotting against him.

Instead of illuminating Cleopatra's feelings, Mankiewicz distracts viewers with a parade—endless rows of marching bands, Vegas showgirls caked with Nefertiti eyeliner, muscular Nubian slaves. When Taylor finally appears—riding atop Cleopatra's gaudy float—she looks like a stupefied Rose Bowl queen. Her son stands by her with an equally vacant expression, as if he were a prop.

Both alone and in crowds, Taylor's talent for intimacy is wasted. The camera rarely lingers on her face. And if she can't show us her face, how can she engage our reptilian brains?

Moving from Egypt to Rome and back again to Egypt, Taylor stumbles helplessly through one huge historically inaccurate set after another. Nearly every set could double as an airplane hanger. The wall frescoes often resemble museum restorations—chipped, broken, faded. Not vibrant and intact, as they would have been in Cleopatra's day.

The queen's final hours oscillate between bathos and parody.

Parody prevails. According to legend, Cleopatra died from the bite of an asp, which was smuggled to her in a basket of figs. Many good ways exist to work this exposition into a scene. Among them, however, is not the approach Mankiewicz took—making an actress renowned for her weight problems grandly proclaim, "First I shall want something to eat."

Critics lambasted the film, but viewers paid no attention. It became the highest grossing film of 1963, earning $22 million. (Unfortunately, it cost $44 million.) Reviewers noted all the film's problems: its overblown scenery, its inadvertently funny script, its over-the-top costumes, its confusing direction. But the *New Statesman* may have come closest to pinpointing its greatest weakness: "Miss Taylor is monotony in a slit skirt, a pre-Christian Elizabeth Arden with sequined eyelids and occasions constantly too large for her."

In fact, the occasions were just right. Taylor had risen to grander, more demanding ones since she was twelve years old. But the sets were too large. No human actress could have filled them.

Recently, *National Geographic* detailed a new quest for the "real" Cleopatra, whom the magazine expects to find in the historical Cleopatra's tomb. In 2004, Kathleen Martinez, an archaeologist from the Dominican Republic, evolved a fresh theory: Cleopatra planned her death as carefully as her life, arranging to be buried in a secret spot outside Alexandria, where her remains and those of Mark Antony were not likely to be disturbed. Octavian, the Roman leader who vanquished

Cleopatra, purportedly buried the couple inside the city. But a conspirator could later have moved their remains.

Martinez's hunch has not yet yielded any mummies. Nor have archaeologists unearthed new images of the queen, whose appearance to this day is a puzzle. (Her only confirmed portrait is a murky profile on a coin.) If Martinez is right, the queen's DNA could resolve many controversies, including whether Cleopatra was of mixed race.

Interesting though the remains could be, they are only part of the "real" Cleopatra, who has lived long past 31 B.C. in myth, music, literature, and art. Between 1540 and 1905, five ballets, forty-five operas, and seventy-seven plays were written about her. She has been portrayed in seven films, including a 1934 effort by Cecil B. DeMille that had even more spectacle and less history than the Burton-Taylor extravaganza. In 2010, producer Scott Rudin announced plans for a new biopic, based on Stacy Schiff's critically acclaimed *Cleopatra: A Life*. Schiff's feminist portrait bodes well for a twenty-first-century Cleopatra. But she may still be overwhelmed by spectacle. Between 3-D, IMAX, and computer-generated imagery, directors today have many more tools with which to distract from story.

Even with the limitations of a 1950s mind-set, Taylor's *Cleopatra* may contain more of the "real" queen than a North African dig. When Taylor's character sneaks into Ceasar's quarters to demand that he make her pharaoh, the "real" Cleopatra emerges. In her ironic counsel to a platoon of ferocious Roman soldiers—"Be not afraid, *I* am with you"—the real Cleopatra comes through. And when she sails her barge to Tarsus so that Antony can meet her on "Egyptian soil," the real Cleopatra appears—cleverly saving face for both herself and the general who would become her lover.

The real Cleopatra doesn't hang around for the full 192 minutes. But she blows in. She flickers. She burns.

"I am fire and air," Shakespeare's Cleopatra says as she prepares for death. And as such she has lived on, not withered by age, in her "infinite variety."

12

1963–1965

IMAGINE BEING ELIZABETH TAYLOR after the release of *Cleopatra*. You and Richard Burton have become the most infamous lovers in the world. Billboards for *Cleopatra* have no writing on them—just a giant image of the two of you in costume. You will never again have privacy. If you ever itch to move among the people, you must move with bodyguards, hidden behind a wig and sunglasses.

You follow Burton to London, where he is set to film *The V.I.P.s*, an updated version of *Grand Hotel*, about a bunch of jet-setters detained in Heathrow Airport by a stubborn fog, which, unlike most obstacles in their lives, they cannot bribe to go away. In real life, Burton is still married to his wife, whom he professes to love, even though he is "in love" with you. You settle into a rooftop suite at the Dorchester Hotel, temporarily shelving your own career.

It is not shelved for long. Anatole de Grunwald, producer of *The V.I.P.s*, offers you $1 million to star opposite Burton—twice what Burton will be paid. You accept.

Burton's $500,000, however, is not nothing. Before *Cleopatra*, the most he ever got for a movie was $125,000. On April 26, 1963, *Time* runs a color painting of Burton on its cover. Inside is an oddly backhanded profile, praising Burton as an actor but suggesting he made a Faustian bargain. His own agent says, "This is a man who sold out." Less hyperbolic, actor Paul Scofield is thus more damning: "Richard professionally is the most interesting actor to have emerged since the war. I think his qualities of heroic presence are not seen to their full advantage in movies. He appears not to be attracted by the best there is in the cinema."

Perhaps in response to such remarks, Burton accepts two classy roles. In *Becket*, he plays Thomas à Becket, the archbishop of Canterbury from 1163 to 1170, who was assassinated after a power struggle with Henry II. In *The Spy Who Came in from the Cold*, a first-rate adaptation of a John Le Carré novel, he portrays Alec Leamas, the anti–James Bond, a burned-out spy, disgusted with his profession's amorality and deceit.

Both you and Burton struggle to be good parents. You adopt a German baby whom you name Maria. You had begun the adoption process when you were married to Fisher. It was one of the things that whipped the Vatican into a froth. Maria has significant congenital health problems, which you spare no expense to correct. "She was spread-eagled in a cast for about two years and we really didn't know whether she would walk ever," you explain. "Finally, a man at Oxford, a great doctor, advised an operation to put in a metal plate. Now she can even run, and she has begun to speak. Her first word was 'Mama.' I guess that's universal, isn't it? But when it happens, you just die."

Through all this—the filming and the parenting and the constant dodging of paparazzi—you search for a project worthy of you and Burton. A project on which you can work together.

In London, you and Burton meet with screenwriter Dalton Trumbo, who has come to discuss *The Sandpiper*, a project sent to you by producer Martin Ransohoff. You don't love the treatment, which was written by Irene and Louis Kamp. But you like Trumbo—and you suggest ways he could enrich the story. You also like your prospective character, Laura Reynolds, a pantheistic rebel with a deep link to nature. The setting, too, appeals to you: Big Sur, California—twenty-six miles south of Pebble Beach. It recalls an innocent time, when you were a twelve-year-old warrior against gender discrimination in *National Velvet*.

As *The Sandpiper* begins to jell, another project also comes together. You are not yet involved, but you will be soon. Warner Brothers pays $500,000 to Edward Albee for the film rights to his Broadway smash, *Who's Afraid of Virginia Woolf?* Jack Warner had intended the movie for Bette Davis and James Mason. The opening line in Albee's play—"What a dump!"—was spoken by Bette Davis in her 1949 movie *Beyond the Forest*. Albee is amused by the thought of Davis doing a deliberate parody of herself, instead of all the inadvertent ones she would later come to do.

You and Burton, however, are bigger stars than Davis and Mason. So the project goes to you. So begins a charmed interlude in your very public life. An interlude in which—whether you are aware of it or not—you introduce millions of viewers to some core elements of feminist thought.

13

The Sandpiper, 1965

The man is a husband and a father and *something else, say a doctor. The woman is a wife and mother* and . . . *nothing. And it's the nothing that kills her.* —Elizabeth Taylor as Laura Reynolds in *The Sandpiper*

As regards the individual nature, woman is defective and misbegotten, for the active power of the male seed tends to the production of a perfect likeness in the masculine sex; while the production of a woman comes from defect in the active power. —Thomas Aquinas, *Summa Theologica,* 1265–1274

Any woman who chooses to behave like a full human being should be warned that the armies of the status quo will treat her as something of a dirty joke. That's their natural and first weapon. —Gloria Steinem, *New York Magazine,* December 20, 1971

T*HE SANDPIPER* BEGINS IN THE SKY above Big Sur, California. From above, we see undulating hills—green and ripe—that suggest the curves of a pregnant woman's body: Mother Nature, the Great Mother, the Mother Goddess. The hills abut the sea, another powerful female symbol. Its waters recall the most primal experience of a human's life—nine months suspended in liquid saline. Then we see a bridge—a triumph of masculine engineering, intended to tame the landscape, which, of course, it can never fully do. The bridge is but a Tinkertoy, a pathetic effort to impose rectilinearity on the heaving, uncontainable earth.

Next we see Laura Reynolds, Taylor's character, as fecund and womanly as the cliffs above her. She is painting at her easel on the beach, having escaped from the patriarchal world into nature, along with her out-of-wedlock, nine-year-old son Danny. Pregnant at age seventeen, she declined to marry her child's father. Nor would she accept her parents' offer of an abortion. She refuses to play by the cruel societal rules that destroyed nearly everybody in *A Place in the Sun*. "I was not abandoned by the father," Reynolds proclaims. "The father was abandoned by me."

Their little paradise, however, is soon despoiled. Her prepubescent son shoots a deer—to see what the "fun" is, or so he explains to the judge to whom the police have delivered him. "Man is the only animal who kills for fun," his mother had told him, and he wanted to understand what she meant. This irritates the judge, who decides that Laura is a bad influence. Fatherless though he is, Danny is still an incipient man, and he must learn to act like one, which includes distancing himself from his mother's antipatriarchal stance.

The judge hands over the boy to Richard Burton, aka Dr. Edward Hewitt, a married Episcopal minister who runs San Simeon, a fancy local prep school. Edward may once have lived by moral principles, but the first thing we see him do is assign a price to his "quality of mercy." If the father of a flunking boy forks over a big gift for a new chapel, Edward won't expel the boy. The deal is brokered by a pillar of the Church, Ward Hendricks, an oily car salesman. All the Church pillars, including the judge, spend their free time in the locker room of the Pebble Beach Golf Links. There, leering and drooling, they speculate on Laura's sexual history, in which Hendricks once played a role. Later, Hendricks will attempt to rape Laura because he feels he is entitled to use her as he pleases.

Poor Laura. Men react to her beauty in the same way that they responded to Taylor's: first with lust, then with snickers. But Edward, to Laura's surprise, seems interested in her thoughts. In his office, he presses her on her religious beliefs.

"I'm a 'Naturalist,'" she asserts. "We believe that man is doomed by his myths. There can be no peace on earth until man rids himself of all belief in the supernatural." Then, realizing that she sounds as dogmatic as a fundamentalist, she adds jokingly, "It's a small sect, with a membership of exactly one—and Danny as a novitiate."

The light tone doesn't drain Laura's resolve to keep Danny out of Edward's parochial school. Even after sheriffs pried him from her home and dragged him to San Simeon, she continues to fight. Finally, though, Edward offers a convincing argument: "We'll give him a set of values that he can rebel against later. Otherwise he might rebel against yours."

Laura and Edward forge a reluctant truce, which holds until Edward commissions her to design some stained-glass windows for his chapel. He doesn't care that she is an atheist.

Neither Diego Rivera nor José Clemente Orozco nor Marc Chagall believed in God, he says, but some of their greatest work is in houses of worship.

Laura's problem, however, is that she doesn't believe in Man. There are no people in the sketches she presents to Edward. She identifies entirely with Nature—pagan, lush, innocent. But "man is essential to any concept of the universe," Edward sputters. For him, "the awe and terror of the infinite universe" is meaningless without a person battling not to fear it. In that moment, I could not help but think of the film's opening panorama, its love note to the immensity of nature. When Laura shows her sketches to Hewitt, she has almost become the landscape. And Edward is the Tinkertoy bridge attempting to contain it.

Well, of course, they have an affair—but it is an affair with conceptual underpinnings. Accused by some critics of having written a shallow sex romp, Dalton Trumbo exploded in a letter to producer Martin Ransohoff: Had Laura "been dull and devoid of ideas, no amount of beauty could have aroused that interest in her as a person which, for a man of Edward's quality, is the only basis from which love can develop. His interest in her as a person—his interest in her ideas and values and way of life—becomes the bait without which he could never have been trapped into a love affair."

Taylor and Burton brought in Trumbo and Michael Wilson, who wrote *A Place in the Sun*, to rethink the script, after Ransohoff, who had come up with the story, showed them a crude early treatment that resembled, Burton said, "a lady's magazine melodrama." Trumbo met with the Burtons in

London and received his marching orders. The couple would bring their luster to the project if it portrayed the complexity of betrayal. Edward should not flee a troubled marriage; he must love his wife but fall in love with Laura. *For her mind.*

This assignment might have daunted a lesser screenwriter, but not Trumbo. From 1950 to 1960, he survived blacklisting and a prison term for refusing to cooperate with the House Un-American Activities Committee. When he was again permitted to work, his acclaimed script for *Spartacus* allowed Kirk Douglas, a muscle-bound scenery chewer, to portray with plausibility the dynamic leader of a Roman slave rebellion. To get inside Laura's head, Trumbo pondered the problems of extreme beauty. He grasped what lustful men and envious women often miss: beauty isolates its possessor and can cause real pain.

In a letter to Ransohoff, he described Laura's retreat to Big Sur: "There came a time when she realized that she must escape from the pressures of that constantly encroaching sea of masculinity, or be drowned in it. Out of this experience came a feeling that she had become no more than a sexual object which attracted the desires and passions of all kinds and classes and ages of men; that no man had ever loved her in the sense that other women are loved, and never would or could; that men, confronted with her, were not capable of loving the woman—only of possessing the object of beauty she represented to them."

Trumbo's meditation made me think of Edith Wharton and her characterization of Lily Bart, the comely, troubled heroine in *The House of Mirth*. "Beauty," Wharton wrote, "needs more tact than the possessor of an average set of features." She will have to manage the desire of men and the envy of other women.

Paganism does not triumph in *The Sandpiper*, but neither does Christianity—which itself is a victory, given the zeal with which monotheists throughout history have struggled to extirpate the Goddess. Edward senses the dryness of his faith; he is a "sloganeer" and fund-raiser. But he is not yet prepared to abandon either Church or wife. So he strikes out alone (as we all are at birth and in death) to find himself. Laura, too, has been awakened by the affair—to the possibility of male tenderness. Still skeptical, but with less reluctance, she lets her son stay in boarding school, hopeful that he can learn the ways of men without becoming a brute.

I am not proud of this, but I loved watching Claire, Edward's wife, disintegrate. As her upscale, patriarchal universe imploded, I felt happy and alive. As she lurched, ashen, from the family station wagon—shattered by Edward's betrayal—I sensed a weight lift off my heart. I couldn't help it. In the majority of post–World War II Hollywood movies, the Claires of the world—conformist, antiseptic helpmates—always win. They get the man, the money, the prize. In contrast, the Lauras—brazen, sexual freethinkers—get their comeuppance: either commitment to an insane asylum or, if they're lucky, death.

In fairness, Edward's wife, portrayed by Eva Marie Saint, is not as bad as most Claires. She's stunted, of course, from all those years of chirpy servitude, and she wears her pastel knits as if the hangers were still inside them. But she isn't vengeful or frigid. Trumbo gave the Burtons what they had requested: Edward isn't escaping a gorgon; he's running *toward* Laura.

My exhilaration at Claire's defeat, I suspect, had less to do with Saint in *The Sandpiper,* and more to do with other, smugger Claires that she portrayed. One of the worst was in *Raintree County,* the ghastly movie that Taylor made after her fantastic turn as Leslie Benedict in *Giant.* Saint's character, named Nell, is in love with Montgomery Clift's character, John, an abolitionist. As you can imagine, Taylor's character, a bombshell named Susanna, quickly steals John away from Nell. But Susanna doesn't get to keep him. She's bad and must therefore suffer a Hollywood reprimand. Like clockwork, Susanna first goes eye-rolling, gibberish-spouting nuts. Then, realizing her chronic Mrs. Rochester impersonation might impede her husband's political career, she does what any noble wife would do: she drowns herself in a swamp. Nell, who has been circling, vulture-like, since the opening credits, can now take her "rightful" place beside John.

The Sandpiper, with all its flaws, seemed a feminist *Citizen Kane.* Not everyone, however, felt this way. Men who liked seeing strong women punished were annoyed. The film "uses the formidable Miss Taylor to rationalize values and views that are immature, specious, meretricious and often ridiculous," Bosley Crowther huffed in the *New York Times.*

Mad magazine, the cultural barometer I myself favored as a kid, mocked the movie's gaps in logic. If Laura is a starving artist, how can she afford to live on some of the most expensive beachfront property in California? *Mad* suggests that

Taylor looks atypically androgynous in a wardrobe test for *National Velvet*.

A cameraman greets Taylor, portraying Velvet Brown, before the Grand National Steeplechase.

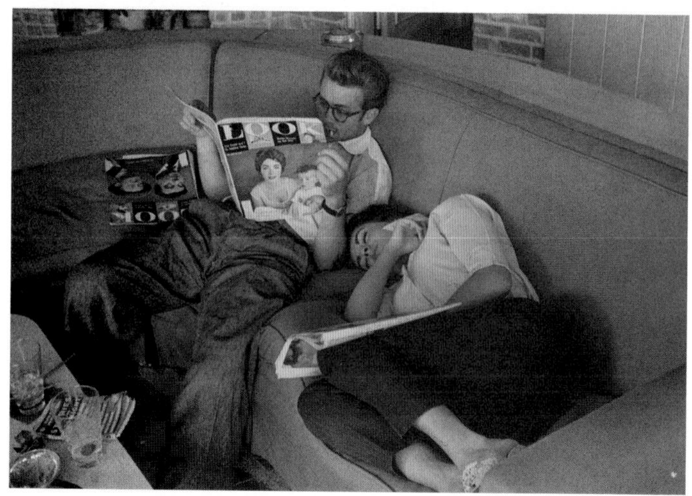

Sleeping *Giant*: James Dean and Taylor relax between takes. Taylor is justifiably exhausted: Her character is the moral anchor of the movie. (Taylor and her new daughter, Liza Todd, are on *Look* magazine's cover.)
(Reprinted with permission of the Richard C. Miller Estate)

Rock Hudson's character is flattened in *Giant*, after raising his fists in support of racial justice. Taylor's character transformed him from a bigot into a humanitarian.
(*Giant* © Giant Productions. Licensed by Warner Bros. Entertainment Inc. All Rights Reserved.)

In *Suddenly, Last Summer,* Taylor's character is trapped on a catwalk above the inmates in an insane asylum: a metaphor for celebrity? (*Suddenly, Last Summer* © 1960, renewed 1988 Horizon Pictures (G.B.) Ltd. All Rights Reserved. Courtesy of Columbia Pictures.)

While filming *Suddenly, Last Summer*, Taylor stands near a symbol of the institution that accused her of "erotic vagrancy." (*Suddenly, Last Summer* © 1960, renewed 1988 Horizon Pictures (G.B.) Ltd. All Rights Reserved. Courtesy of Columbia Pictures.)

In *BUtterfield 8*, Taylor's character refuses to be rented or owned. She scrawls "No Sale" on her married lover's mirror.

In London, crowds struggle to glimpse Taylor after her tracheotomy and resurrection.

At the 1963 London premiere of *Cleopatra*, as on the billboard in New York's Times Square, no names were needed to identify the stars. (© Terry Disney/Hulton-Deutsch Collection/Corbis)

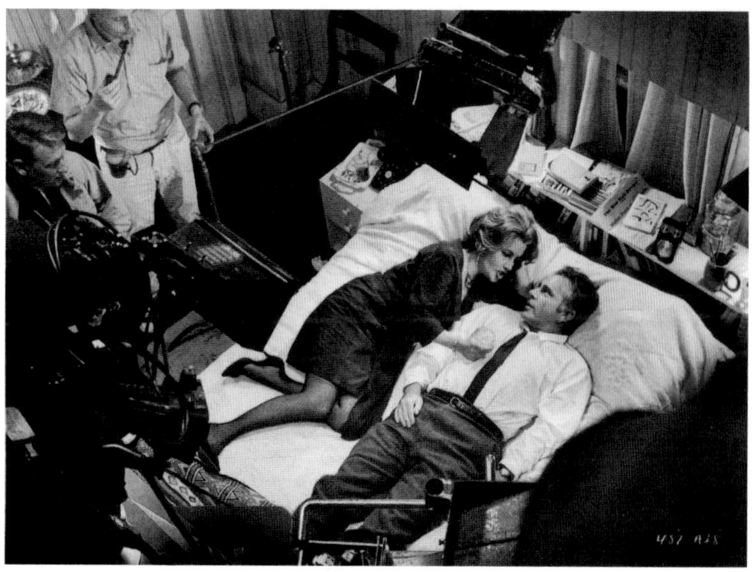

In *Who's Afraid of Virginia Woolf?*, Taylor and Burton share a moment of Hollywood-style intimacy: surrounded by lights, cameras, and recording equipment.

(*Who's Afraid of Virginia Woolf?* © Warner Bros. Pictures, Inc. All Rights Reserved.)

To the confusion of their guests—a new faculty member and his wife—George (Burton) aims a rifle at Martha (Taylor), who cackles diabolically when it fires. The trick gun contains an umbrella.

(*Who's Afraid of Virginia Woolf?* © Warner Bros. Pictures, Inc. All Rights Reserved.)

Liz Smith said Taylor often helped "a bird with a wing down"—like this feathered costar from *The Sandpiper*.

No love was lost between Taylor and playwright Lillian Hellman in Austin Pendleton's 1981 production of *The Little Foxes*. Also shown are Maureen Stapleton and Tom Aldredge.
(© Time & Life Pictures/Getty Images)

perhaps because Laura models nude and favors scanty beachwear, she has saved a lot of money on clothes.

I expected this fixation on Taylor's looks from *Mad*, but not from my friend Jeffrey, a scholar of mathematics, computer science, and religion, whose opinion I frequently seek on all manner of subjects. After urging him to watch the movie, I asked whether he thought Laura had weakened Edward's faith. No question, he said, then described a scene where she poses naked for a sculptor: "When I saw her, *I* forgot about God."

Even Pauline Kael fixed on the nudity—likely threatened by Taylor's beauty: "Taylor demurely cups her breasts with her hands, though they seem inadequate to the task." In fairness, the scene really was a little strange. The Production Code Administration forbade Taylor to conceal her breasts with her bare hands; instead she covered them with what look like black cocktail napkins.

With decades of distance from the real-life Burtons and their infamy as a couple, it's easier to see Laura and Edward as fictive characters. Viewed in this way, the film dramatizes a phenomenon that Leonard Shlain would detail three decades later in his groundbreaking book, *The Alphabet Versus the Goddess: The Conflict Between Word and Image.*

Shlain drew on brain anatomy, anthropology, and history to make a startling suggestion: that literacy may have a dark side. The very act of reading, Shlain says, prioritizes the left hemisphere of the brain, which processes linear, abstract, and masculine thought. It deemphasizes the right side, which is visual, holistic, and feminine. Over time, the ascendancy of the left brain has led to many bad things: the denigration of women, the banning of imagery from churches, and patriarchal domination.

As Shlain tells it, the values that typify the right brain are "empathy with the plight of one's companions, generosity toward strangers, tolerance of dissent, love of nature, nurturance of children, laughter, playfulness, mysticism, forgiveness of enemies, and nonviolence." In contrast, the left brain valorizes "work, goals, focus, power, and money." These are of course good things; the left brain is not evil. But it does tend to frown on obstacles to its ambitions. Hence its other attributes: "cruelty, argument, a disregard for nature, and a lack of concern for the lame and the halt"—all the things that make one "a successful hunter/killer."

Shlain's most astonishing suggestion is that the content of a spoken message is transformed when it is committed to print. The Gospels that contain the words of Jesus Christ, for instance, overwhelmingly accentuate the values of the right brain. "There is not a single incident where Jesus or His Apostles ever murdered, banished, burned or imprisoned anyone," Shlain observes. Yet hierarchical and sexist institutions sprang up as soon as those spoken words were written down.

In *The Sandpiper*, Laura Reynolds is all right brain—intuitive, nurturing, visual. She expresses herself in pictures. Edward is all left brain. Although he sermonizes well, he remains very much the product of his culture, which prioritizes writing. We see this when he disciplines a boy who defaced a wall with an obscenity. The punishment: "Learn the equivalent words in German, French, and Latin. Then decline each noun and conjugate each verb in all tenses including the subjunctive." Alone, Laura and Edward are fractured; together, like the hemispheres of the brain, they become powerful and complete.

When Laura left home to have her out-of-wedlock son, she broke free from left-brain culture. She rejected all its hallmarks: male supremacy, chronic conflict, and verbal one-upmanship. In Taylor's next film, however, she plays a character who made the opposite choice; who uses words like daggers, who accepts the inferiority of women, and whose right brain seems to have atrophied from disuse.

This next film—*Who's Afraid of Virginia Woolf?*—can be viewed as a bookend to *The Sandpiper,* or as the flip side of a coin. After a balmy, enveloping West Coast interlude, this film takes us to the cold and brittle East. Another day, another skirmish—all, in Edward Albee's words, "blood under the bridge."

14

Who's Afraid of Virginia Woolf? 1966

The adjusted or cured ones who live without conflict or anxiety in the confined world of home have forfeited their own being; the others, the miserable frustrated ones, still have some hope. —Betty Friedan, *The Feminine Mystique*, 1963

The famous problem of the movie's frank language turns out to be no problem at all. There is too much genuine excitement present for one even to pay any attention to the four-letter words. I was hardly conscious of their presence. —Richard Schickel, *Life*, July 22, 1966

I'm loud and I'm vulgar and I wear the pants in this house because somebody has to. But I'm not a monster. —Elizabeth Taylor as Martha in *Who's Afraid of Virginia Woolf?*

EVERY TIME I watch this movie—and I have viewed it more than a dozen times—I notice something new. Often it's an insight or a turn of phrase from playwright Edward Albee's script. And I do mean Albee. During the adaptation process, Mike Nichols, the film's director, and Ernest Lehman, its producer and screenwriter, made a tough decision: not to subject Albee's language to the Production Code meat grinder.

More frequently, though, I pick up on a nonverbal detail—a grunt, a gesture, or a tic—evidence that Elizabeth Taylor and Richard Burton are not merely reciting Albee's lines. They are inhabiting his characters: Martha, the fifty-two-year-old daughter of a university president, and George, her husband, six years younger and an associate professor of history at the school of which her father is president.

The film's opening sequence is striking. Late one autumn night on a quaint New England campus, George and Martha wobble home from a party. The vastness of the grounds—the ancient, sturdy trees—underscore the oppressiveness of their cluttered, dingy house, where most of the action will take place.

Martha's gait speaks volumes. It is unsteady, but not solely because she is drunk. She hesitates before placing her weight on her foot, then springs forward haltingly, as if she were walking on a hot stove. Most women will recognize the source of her torment: a long night in high heels.

Martha's laugh fractures the night. It is guttural, booming—deeper than her reedy voice. She is momentarily happy. At the party, she had cracked a successful joke, replacing "big bad wolf" with "Virginia Woolf" in the refrain of a nursery rhyme.

I doubt Albee's allusion to Woolf was accidental. *Three Guineas*, Woolf's handy guide to women's oppression in Edwardian England, talks about the demoralization experienced by "daughters of educated men"—bright women denied formal schooling and forced to express themselves through their husbands' careers and children. In the best of circumstances, this arrangement is stultifying. In less-than-perfect conditions—when, for example, the husband is a failure and the couple cannot have children—the arrangement can be hell on earth.

Martha is the quintessential educated man's daughter; her father runs the university. George is the archetypal failure; at midlife, he has not reached the rank of full professor. But the biggest tragedy—the bottomless well from which Martha draws her bitterness—is her inability to bear children. George may have been the partner with the infertility problems. But in the 1960s, this didn't matter. Women were always to blame. Martha is—to use a cruel, dated adjective that made me flinch when I read it in a review—"barren."

When the couple arrives back at their house, Martha runs to the refrigerator and shoves a chicken leg into her mouth. This is a reaction to the way women are expected to eat at parties—demurely, so they don't spill clam dip down their décolletage, and daintily, so they never get enough to satisfy their hunger.

Although it is after midnight, Martha has invited guests for a nightcap: Nick, a cocky new member of the biology department, and Honey, his dowdy heiress wife. As portrayed by George Segal, Nick is a muscular ex-athlete who bursts with ambition—as does his suit, which appears to be a size too small. He expects to rise at the university by, among other things, "plowing pertinent" faculty wives, like, say, Martha.

One nightcap turns into many. George and Martha lead the younger couple though a night of sadomasochistic games.

Sandy Dennis, portraying Honey, throws up a lot. And when dawn finally puts an end to their savagery, all four have had their darkest, most humiliating secrets exposed.

I liked this movie when I first saw it in college in the late 1970s. But I don't think I fully understood it until now. Back then, I believed that feminism had delivered me from all aspects of Martha's fate. It had pried open the gates of my ivy-covered school, which ten years earlier had been barred against women. Life was a dessert cart of opportunities; the women of my generation would be able to sample them all.

This is, of course, impossible. But one does not realize this until middle age—another subject of Albee's play. Each opportunity taken represents another that was lost. To have no regrets is to have made no choices.

George has many regrets—possibly more than Martha. And he may have suffered more than she from the tyranny of patriarchy. He has certainly suffered at the hands of Martha's father, who robbed him of something as precious as a child: his creative expression. The old man forbade him to publish an autobiographical novel whose content may (or may not) have embarrassed the university. His creativity is thwarted—bottled up—stuffed down. It has no outlet besides toxic wordplay.

To me, the film's feminist message could not have been more explicit. Patriarchy crushes men and women alike. But reviewers at the time did not seem to notice this, and some projected their own paranoia onto the movie.

In the *New Yorker*, Edith Oliver, who admired the film, discerned an important difference between the play and the movie: Lehman excised many of George's hints that Martha had had an incestuous relationship with her father. To me, such trims buttress the feminist point: Martha is not pathologically attached to her own father, but to the idea of an all-powerful father—the cornerstone of patriarchy. In *Life* magazine, critic Richard Schickel recognized the range in Taylor's portrayal of Martha—the way she moves from "comic stridency" to "the desperation of the mortally wounded." He added that Taylor "fully deserves all the praise she will inevitably receive."

But the reviewer for *Time*—protected by the magazine's convention of unsigned articles—used his platform for a bizarre misogynistic rant. His word choices suggest a fear and hatred of women. Instead of recognizing Martha's pathos, he only saw the threat that she posed to men. He dehumanized her through caricature, terming her "an aging maneater" who has "a father fixation and a casual lust for younger chaps." To the reviewer for *Newsweek*—also protected by anonymity—the movie was a pretext for a deranged, homophobic tantrum. Because Albee is a gay man, the critic reasoned, he could never possibly understand either heterosexuals or love. Albee "has not really written about men and women, with a potential for love and sex," the reviewer sneered. He has used "his harrowing heterosexual couples as surrogates for homosexual partners having a vicious, narcissistic, delightedly self-indulgent spat."

I wish Ernest Lehman and Mike Nichols had defeated the Production Code Administration in some huge climactic battle—similar to the clashes in the movie. But by 1966, the

Administration was no longer an invincible monolith. It merely needed a push from a feather to make it collapse.

Geoffrey Shurlock, however, the head censor, decided to withhold approval from *Who's Afraid of Virginia Woolf?* according to the letter of the law, even though he himself liked the movie. "I think it's a marvelous film," he told *Life*. He did this to avoid the embarrassment he had experienced in 1964, when, because of director Billy Wilder's revered status in the entertainment community, Shurlock had approved Wilder's *Kiss Me, Stupid*—a tacky sex romp that earned a C rating—the lowest of the low—from the Catholic Legion of Decency.

When Warner Brothers submitted Lehman's script to Shurlock's office, it got back a five-page list of words and phrases that needed to be cut. They included "goddam," "screw you," "bugger," "plowing pertinent wives," "hump the hostess," and "mount her like a goddam dog." Most of this language has remained in the finished picture. Warner Brothers appealed Shurlock's decision to the Motion Picture Association of America Production Code Review Board—the same group that Sam Spiegel had petitioned in 1959 with *Suddenly, Last Summer.* This time, however, the review board didn't just rubber stamp the film. It concocted a new way of handling "mature" subject matter: refusing theater admission to people under eighteen years of age.

Meanwhile, the Legion of Decency—which by 1966 had rechristened itself the National Catholic Office for Motion Pictures—recoiled from imposing an unpopular directive on the Church's increasingly rebellious flock. Instead, it recruited eighty-one volunteers—college-educated Catholics who liked movies—to determine what it should do about the film. Most thought *Who's Afraid of Virginia Woolf?* had redeeming artistic value, though a minority could not get beyond its language. "The only possible favorable comment I can make is that the actors ably depict the varying moods of drunken persons," a dissenter observed.

Having discerned which way the wind was blowing, the Church signed off on *Whose Afraid of Virginia Woolf?* Mature adults, it felt, could handle the material—as long as such adults first asked the Church permission to be allowed to handle it.

The verdict came as a relief to Nichols. "Disguising profanity with clean but suggestive phrases is really dirtier," he told an interviewer. "It reminds me of an old Gary Cooper movie when somebody said, 'He's so poor he hasn't got a pot to put flowers in.' Everybody in the audience got what was intended: echoes of wild talk, it seems to me, are deliberately titillating."

Lehman, too, was relieved. His experience adapting *Virginia Woolf* was a far cry from the one he had had with the previous play he brought from Broadway to the screen: *The Sound of Music.*

Many people have favorite scenes in *Who's Afraid of Virginia Woolf?* Mine embodies what I like most about the movie—its dark comedy, its zany yet resonant non sequiturs. The scene occurs near the end of the film, after Martha consummated her attraction to Nick. She sits alone on the front porch. George has momentarily vanished. Nick returns from a successful search for his missing wife, Honey. When he last saw her, hours earlier, she had been retching in the bathroom. He wishes his search had failed.

"My wife's in the can with a liquor bottle and she winks at me," Nick, stunned, tells Martha. "She's lying down on the floor on the tiles all curled up. And she starts peeling the label on the liquor bottle, the brandy bottle—"

With a look of genuine concern, Martha cuts him off. Even on a night like this, she has not forgotten how to be a hostess: "Maybe she'd be more comfortable in the tub," she suggests.

At first I thought this line was the funniest in the film, because Taylor plays it sweetly, rather than for laughs. But it may, in fact, be the saddest—far more wrenching than Martha's later breakdown, her frank admission of her fears.

Being a good hostess is all that Martha has in her life—all she has ever allowed herself to have. She is the daughter of an educated man. A handmaiden to educated men. A woman who has never questioned the primacy of educated men or their arid left-brain values.

In this instant, though, something stirs in the withered right hemisphere of Martha's brain. Something empathetic. Something that may one day deliver her from the self-imposed combat zone where she and George currently reside.

15

1967–1973

IF *I LOVE LUCY* had been written in iambic pentameter—and lit without shadows, as if it were an Italian Renaissance painting—it would resemble the Burtons' 1967 version of *The Taming of the Shrew.* The film is packed with physical comedy—pratfalls—and domestic skirmishes worthy of professional wrestling. Its most essential element, of course, is its feminist spin, which is in large part conveyed visually. Franco Zeffirelli, the film's director, achieves this by having his actors behave in a way that contradicts what they are saying.

Most people know Shakespeare's play; it's a staple of high school English classes. They may not recall pretty Bianca or her schoolmaster beau, but they remember Katerina, the so-called shrew (aka "bonny Kate" and "Kate the curst"), and Petruchio, the blustering fortune hunter who allegedly tames her. They also remember Kate's capitulation speech near the end of the play. This speech—and whether it is delivered with irony or in earnest—determines the meaning of the entire play.

The Burtons originated the project and brought on Zeffirelli, primarily an opera director, to create its look. He built the town of Padua, where the play is set, inside the Dino De

Laurentiis studios, about twenty miles south of Rome. To achieve the absence of shadows, the production team had to "skirt every pan"—which is to say, hang a cloth around each overhead light, to diffuse the illumination and thus eliminate patches of shade. (Burton enlisted Richard McWhorter, who had produced *The Spy Who Came in from the Cold*, as production manager; McWhorter himself saw to the labor-intensive details.)

Depending upon how it's acted, the play can tell different stories. It can be about two harsh people who soften because they fall in love. Or it can be about a thug who brutalizes a woman into submission.

In the Burtons' version, Kate and Petruchio fall in love. Taylor delivers Kate's famous capitulation speech without irony. This was her decision, Zeffirelli says in his memoir. But what happens after the speech (in which she tells wives to "serve, love and obey") belies her words. Kate's seeming submission permitted Petruchio to win a bet. And when he should have been lingering with his friends to gloat over his triumph, he instead appears stricken. He realizes: Kate left the room. He dashes after her. Without Kate, he is confused and bereft. Visually, the message is clear: Kate is *utterly* in control; wherever she goes, Petruchio will slavishly follow.

Viewed in this context, Kate's speech is not an exhortation to surrender, but a strategy for converting an antagonist to one's point of view—the same strategy that Leslie Benedict used to gain control of the Benedict household and ensure that her ideas lived on in the Benedict children. "I am ashamed that women are so simple," Kate says. "To offer war where they should kneel for peace." In other words, diplomacy works. Open antagonism doesn't, making it both foolish and useless: "Our lances are but straws."

Like *The Taming of the Shrew*, Taylor's next film, *Reflections in a Golden Eye,* has an impressive pedigree. It was based on a novel by Carson McCullers, adapted by Chapman Mortimer and Gladys Hill, and directed by John Huston. McCullers loved the script: "You have made my original book a new and powerful creation," she wrote to Huston, Mortimer, and Hill. The film explores the stifling effect of rigid gender roles in an epicenter of male supremacy: a U.S. Army post in the South, where, we learn at the opening of the film, a murder will be committed. The puzzle: who will kill whom?

On this army base, all the gentle, artsy, right-brain types either go mad, kill themselves, run away, or receive unexpected military discharges. The dim and brutal ones thrive. Taylor's character, Leonora, is so dim that she can barely write a letter. She is, however, beautiful and voraciously heterosexual. When her gruff, hypermasculine husband, Major Penderton, portrayed by Marlo Brando, rejects her, we have no doubt that he is homosexual. Penderton is also a voyeur—besotted with a handsome enlisted man whom he spies upon, and who, in turn, is besotted with and spies upon Leonora. Robert Forster, a twenty-three-year old newcomer, played Private Williams.

In 1967, Gloria Steinem was not yet a feminist icon. She was a journalist and a friend of the film's producer, Ray Stark. In a note to Stark, Steinem expressed amazement at

Taylor's willingness to subsume herself in the project: "What other movie queen would have—or does now—take such un-Hollywood-like chances with her glamour? She probably knows less about Stanislavsky than Natalie Wood does, yet she became old and fat for Virginia Woolf and now tops it off with being simple-minded as Leonora."

Huston shot most of the film outside Rome in the De Laurentiis studios. He demanded a closed set for intense scenes, such as the one where Leonora strips for Penderton, then mocks him for his unresponsiveness. When Huston began filming this scene, all nonessential crew had apparently been banished. But when Taylor's naked body-double climbed a flight of stairs, the crew reappeared. "More guys than you can imagine," Forster recalls with amusement, "popping out from under trucks and behind tires—all the places they had hidden."

The press, however, was effectively excluded, creating a protected atmosphere that encouraged actors to take risks. As Williams, Forster had to ride naked on Leonora's horse, while Penderton, hiding, gapes at him. In response to the safe atmosphere, Forster sent away his body double: "My pride took over, and I said, 'I'm not gonna let that guy be me,'" he said. "The next thing I know, the wardrobe department hands me a flesh jock strap without the straps and a roll of flesh covered tape"—which Forster tried to wear—until the objects fell off, and he boldly completed the scene without them.

The closed set, however, put a damper on prerelease publicity. To promote the film, Steinem encouraged Stark to play up the surprising way in which Taylor had evolved as an actress: "She is expert at what she does, professional on the set, un-catty in her work relationships with other actresses, and pretty much willing to try whatever the director asks. All of this runs contrary to the public image of a spoiled and difficult *La Taylor.* And so does the fact that she took a salary cut in order to get Brando on the film."

Reflections in a Golden Eye did poorly at the box office. Viewers didn't warm to its southern Gothic sensibility or its implication that beneath the exterior of a fearsome army officer, a hurt gay man might lurk. "Hell hath no fury like a homosexual scorned," Bosley Crowther wrote in the *New York Times.* Although Brando's character is far from heroic, viewers today would be hard-pressed not to recognize his pathos. He is so brainwashed by society's expectations of manliness that he cannot accept who he is.

I think the film is among Taylor's best from this period. Her collaborations with Burton were not so great. During the golden age of European avant-garde cinema—when the art houses burst with smart, visually enticing work—the Burtons had a knack for finding bad art films and starring in them. Burton's low-budget version of Christopher Marlowe's *Doctor Faustus* adapted by his Cambridge buddy, Nevill Coghill, may have been the worst. Taylor appears in it as Helen of Troy, but she has no lines—because a speaking part would have cost too much.

After *The Taming of the Shrew*, Burton retained McWhorter, a Hollywood veteran, to produce his films. McWhorter soldiered through *Doctor Faustus*, but when Burton brought him the script for *Boom!*—an adaptation of a Tennessee Williams flop—he resigned. "Until you get ready to make a picture where I can be of some service," he told Burton. "I'm wasting your money and my time."

Boom! moved forward anyway, with Joseph Losey directing. The film has fans (including director John Waters), but it strains credibility. Burton is supposed to be a young hustler—despite the fact that he looks old enough to be Taylor's father. And Taylor is supposed to be a woman—despite her Kabuki drag and a name usually applied to effeminate men: "Sissy."

In real life, Taylor doesn't project ambiguous sexuality; she clearly likes men. But two of her next projects—*Secret Ceremony* for Losey, and *X, Y and Zee* for director Brian G. Hutton—required her to flirt with bisexuality. This was not a success. *X, Y and Zee*, however, written by Irish novelist Edna O'Brien and set in 1960s London, at least had a clever premise: a scheming wife (Taylor) connives to wrest her husband (Michael Caine) away from his mistress (Susannah York) by seducing the mistress herself. Taylor gamely—and plausibly—goes to bed with York, who is supposed to convey enthusiasm. But York looks like rigor mortis has set in, undermining the premise.

In 1968, Taylor ceased to be among the top-ten box-office stars. This was a very big deal for Taylor. Biographers agree: it shook her confidence. Her plunge continued in 1970 with *The Only Game in Town*, a painful coda to the luminous career of director George Stevens. Promoted with the tag line "Dice was his vice. Men hers," the movie promised a camp fest to rival *Boom!* But I felt sad when I watched it. In *A Place in the Sun* and *Giant*, Stevens had taken on big themes and created rich worlds. In *The Only Game in Town*, his epic style merely accentuated the pettiness of the characters and the tedium of their story.

As a couple, the Burtons retained their luster. In 1968, when Burton gave Taylor the 33.19-carat Krupp diamond, the story was front-page news. But their projects became increasingly dull. Their 1973 venture, *Divorce His Divorce Hers*, "holds all the joy of standing by at an autopsy," *Variety* wrote.

Ash Wednesday, Taylor's next film, broke this pattern—for her alone, not Burton. It did not lift her significantly higher, but it slowed her fall.

16

Ash Wednesday, 1973

HARD TO BELIEVE, but in 1973, the brows of most middle-aged women furrowed when they frowned. Neither Botox nor dermal filler nor facelifts were commonplace. In the opening scenes of *Ash Wednesday*, Elizabeth Taylor, made up to look dowdy, portrays Barbara Sawyer, the fifty-something wife of a rich midwestern lawyer, who enters a Swiss clinic to undergo extensive cosmetic surgery.

Documentary-style, with no underscore, *Ash Wednesday* lays out what such surgery involves—to a public not yet accustomed to reading in fashion magazines about eyelifts, nose jobs, and chemical peels. Barbara's "aged" face occupies the entire screen, as a real-life plastic surgeon (not an actor) draws lines where he will make incisions. The camera lingers on her crepey eyelids and the folds of her upper neck. Shouting "cut" and "sponge" in French to his assistants, the surgeon slices into her flesh, rearranges it, and sews it back up. In the 1970s, TV medical shows didn't depict the gore of surgery. *Ash Wednesday*, in contrast, shocked viewers with footage of an actual facelift—not Taylor's but that of a woman who looked similar to her.

We next see Barbara—and the clinic's other patients—with mummylike bandages around their heads. Her face is a patchwork of eggplant bruises; her upper lip is black. When the bandages come off, however, we understand why she took the trouble: She now looks like Elizabeth Taylor. Barbara hopes her rejuvenated appearance will win back her husband, who has fallen for a younger woman. But after the surgery, while vacationing at Cortina d'Ampezzo, a posh Alpine ski resort where she had expected to meet her husband, she remains miserable, indifferent to the scenery and bonhomie around her. Her husband refuses to join her—dashing her hope of rekindling their romance. Nor can even she appreciate her own beauty if he doesn't value it.

By the end of the movie, however, with the encouragement of her independent, feminist daughter (who is defiantly oblivious to fashion) and a worldly gay photographer whom she met at the clinic, Barbara begins to discover . . . herself. She doesn't need the pathetic husband whose terror of aging propels him into the arms of younger women. She has her looks and (unless she really bungles the divorce) his money.

The movie shows both what plastic surgery can repair (the grosser ravages of age) and what it can't (a bad marriage). The movie's message is feminist, but not in a simpleminded way. It doesn't condemn surgery per se; it cautions against doing it for the wrong reasons. Barbara underwent pain and risk to please someone other than herself; this made her a doormat. She also internalized society's objectification of women; she saw herself only as a withered old thing.

For the right reasons, however, cosmetic surgery can be

empowering. It won't mend a broken marriage or stave off death. But it will rescue a healthy person—aware that he or she is more than just an object—from having to endure the shock of a liver-spotted stranger in the mirror.

Burton hated the movie, and in a 1973 letter to his assistants (sold at auction in 2004), he called it "a fucking lousy nothing bloody film." This seems extreme. At worst it is harmless melodrama. What got to him, I suspect, was the portrait of Barbara's husband, played by Henry Fonda—a clownish old goat chasing the fountain of youth in a woman less than half his age.

During the filming of *Ash Wednesday*, "Lumpy" and "Pockface"—as Taylor and Burton referred to each other—grew apart. They divorced on June 26, 1974, only to remarry on October 10, 1975. This reconciliation, however, did not prevent Burton from taking up with Suzy Hunt, a model more than twenty years his junior. So on July 29, 1976, Taylor and Burton again divorced. This time they meant it.

In 1974, Taylor made another flawed but engaging movie, *The Driver's Seat*, based on a novella by Muriel Spark. Campy and erratic, the film flirts with a macabre sort of female power: Taylor plays a woman searching for a man she can induce to murder her. But her next project, a film version of Stephen Sondheim's *A Little Night Music*, directed by Harold Prince, was cringeworthy. Much of the film's funding came from Austria, so the producers set the story there instead of in Sweden, where the Broadway musical and the Ingmar Bergman movie on which it was based took place. The plot climaxes on a summer night when the sun seemingly never sets—a phenomenon that occurs strikingly at Sweden's northern latitude (and not so much in Austria).

The film tanked. And by 1976, Taylor had become as tired of movies as Cousin Sebastian (in *Suddenly, Last Summer*) had once been of blondes. She needed a new role to display her talents: political wife. I will not dwell on Taylor in the 1970s, because her life was in transition. She should have had a chrysalis in which to change—from which she could have dramatically emerged. According to 12-step literature, a person must "hit bottom" before he or she can recover. Taylor began a swift slide toward that destination on December 24, 1976, when she married John Warner, an authoritarian, antifeminist Republican who would use her celebrity to advance his political career. (In fairness, the future U.S. senator had at least one thing going for him: he was very handsome.)

Warner served as secretary of the navy, but he gained his wealth through a strategic marriage. His Georgetown house and 2,700-acre farm were spoils from his divorce from Catherine Mellon, daughter of philanthropist Paul Mellon. From the get-go, his politics and Taylor's were at odds. In 1960, he campaigned for Richard M. Nixon; Taylor supported John F. Kennedy. In 1976, he worked for Gerald Ford; Taylor backed Jimmy Carter. But when Warner ran for the Senate in Virginia, Taylor found herself in what could not have been an easy spot: campaigning for a candidate who opposed much of what she believed in. This included the Equal Rights Amendment.

"I'm sure Taylor did support the Equal Rights Amendment," syndicated gossip columnist Liz Smith, a longtime friend of Taylor, told me in 2009. "During her marriage to Warner, they actually had a public argument concerning women's issues, employment. Please forgive me, it was 1980, and I just don't remember the details. But I do remember Warner put his hand up to silence her—he was embarrassed—and she said something like, 'Don't you raise that all-commanding domineering hand to me!' Of course, this was as much acting-out as 'Elizabeth Taylor' as it was her feminism kicking in."

Warner lost the election. Weirdly, though, the winner was killed in a freak airplane accident. So Warner and Taylor campaigned again, and on November 7, 1977, Warner squeaked in—by less than one percentage point.

Kate Burton, Richard's daughter, has a warm memory of visiting Taylor and Warner at Warner's Virginia home—long after Taylor and her father had divorced. Burton was an undergraduate at Brown University, and she had traveled to Washington, D.C., to attend a campaign rally for Warner. She remembers the event as "a hoot." Burton had never been to the American South before. And the idea of her cosmopolitan former stepmother "in this southern mansion making fried chicken was so incongruous to me." Nevertheless, Taylor made her feel "very welcome." And she thought Taylor seemed happy.

Burton was, however, alone in this perception. Taylor may not yet have hit bottom, but she was getting close. In her 1987 diet book, Taylor owned up to having gained fifty pounds: "Eating became one of the most pleasant activities I could find to fill the lonely hours and I ate and drank with abandon.

When I gained weight, I just bought more clothes." She and Warner drifted apart: "John went his way and I went mine. He headed for the Senate; I zeroed into self-destruction." She dared not even open the funny pages for distraction. *Doonesbury* cartoonist Garry Trudeau attacked her viciously and repeatedly as "the wife of some dim dilettante who managed to buy, marry, and luck his way into the U.S. Senate."

Clichés often contain some truth. It *is* always darkest before the dawn. And after you hit bottom, the only way to go is up. In 1980, exiled in what she termed the "domestic Siberia" of a senator's wife, Taylor met Zev Buffman, producer of a revival of *Brigadoon* at Washington's National Theatre. After the performance, she confided that she had always longed to do live theater, and Buffman, being no fool, leaped to give her a chance. They discussed many possible vehicles, narrowing the choices to Noël Coward's *Hay Fever* and Lillian Hellman's *The Little Foxes*.

Taylor's downward slide was over. She was slowly climbing back. *The Little Foxes* would gain her a great deal of ground.

17

The Little Foxes, 1981

I'm going to be alive and have what I want. —Elizabeth Taylor as Regina Hubbard Giddens to her ailing husband in *The Little Foxes*

I'M NOT PROJECTING FEMINISM onto Austin Pendleton's version of *The Little Foxes.* He admits to having put it there. In 1981, when Zev Buffman asked him to direct Elizabeth Tayor in a revival of Lillian Hellman's 1937 play, he didn't immediately say yes. He thought about the lead role—Regina Hubbard Giddens—and how Taylor might distinguish her Regina from the memorable Reginas of the past.

In William Wyler's 1941 movie, Bette Davis played Regina as a cartoon villainess. She picked up where Tallulah Bankhead, who had originated the part on Broadway, left off. Likewise, in Mike Nichols's 1967 revival at Lincoln Center, Anne Bancroft interpreted Regina as evil incarnate. But Pendleton—who had played Leo, Regina's dim-witted son, in the 1967 production—saw another explanation for Regina's behavior. And he wanted to explore it.

"What if this woman starts out a different way from how

she ends up?" he mused. "What if she starts out like Elizabeth Taylor—a woman who is naturally sympathetic but who has an enormous appetite for living? And she becomes hardened by all the adversity she encounters, from her husband and brothers, into a woman of greed? She's not a greedy woman at the beginning of the play—she's a woman with an appetite for life."

As Pendleton explained this, a sly smile crossed his otherwise diffident face. He accepted Buffman's offer. And he set a challenge for himself: create a sympathetic Regina; a feminist Regina, a Regina twisted by the cruelty of men.

Pendleton's version of *The Little Foxes* was so blazingly feminist—and, for Taylor, such a restorative force—that even though it can't be seen, it deserves inclusion alongside her most famous movie roles. Of course I can't re-create the experience. Viewers at a live performance don't just gape at the actors. They engage with them: laughing, crying, clapping. And the actors, in turn, pick up on their energy. This crackle of feeling—this neural loop—makes theater thrilling. What I can do, however, is detail the production—as Pendleton did for me in 2008.

The Little Foxes deals with the Hubbard family—turn-of-the-century strivers in the American South. Regina Giddens (née Hubbard) has two greedy brothers, a mentally challenged son, a cloying daughter, an alcoholic aunt, and a passive-aggressive husband—all of whom romanticize their "genteel," slave-owning past. When a Chicago manufacturer scouts land for a factory in the Hubbards' hometown, Regina's brothers start scheming. He is also looking for investors—and a little capital now will likely mean a big fortune later. When Hubbards enter the picture, it will also mean thievery, deceit, backstabbing, and murder.

To play Regina, Taylor needed different skills from the ones she had honed in films. She had to memorize the entire play—not one scene at a time. She had to propel her voice to the back of the theater. At first Pendleton had more confidence in her than she had in herself. "Anyone who could do that sustained, long take at the end of *Suddenly, Last Summer* could be in a play," he said.

Taylor worked hard, he recalled. "And she never once did anything that could remotely be called 'pulling rank.'" This was good, because the other legend on the project—Lillian Hellman—pulled rank all the time. "She and I had the worst fights I've ever had with anyone in a professional situation. We screamed at each other," Pendleton said. "But I absolutely adored her. I miss her to this day."

Hellman's characters were inspired by her own life. Oddly, given Hellman's infamous volatility, she identified with Alexandra, Regina's daughter, a beacon of harmony and peace. She hated the real-life model for Regina and could not see what Pendleton saw in the character. Pendleton kept mum about his feminist spin, lest Hellman try to ax him from the project.

The Little Foxes opened at the Eisenhower Theater in Washington, D.C., four days before President Ronald Reagan was shot. Taylor's Regina was not a one-note gorgon. She was hungry for life—until her vindictive husband and conniving brothers forced her to become a rapacious monster. When Hellman saw the production, Pendleton sensed her displeasure—as did anyone within fifty yards. "This is the worst night of my life," she yelled, angrily banging her cane on the lobby floor.

The play ends with a line that recalls Martha in *Who's Afraid of Virginia Woolf?* Regina has done a very bad thing—a thing that drives her daughter away. But before Alexandra departs, she asks her, "Mama, are you afraid?" And the audience realizes that Regina, like Martha, terrorizes others to subdue her own paralyzing fears.

On May 7, the play opened at the Martin Beck Theatre on Broadway. Critics kvelled. Pendleton's take on the play was a hit. "Miss Taylor is no cardboard harridan," Frank Rich wrote in the *New York Times*. "Regina perfectly taps this actress's special gift—first fully revealed in the film version of 'Who's Afraid of Virginia Woolf?'—for making nastiness stinging and funny at the same time."

Taylor also used her "special gift" offstage. When Hellman told her, "I'm really Alexandra," Taylor replied, "Oh, come on, Lillian. You're Regina."

The tension between Taylor and Hellman traveled with the production to its run in Los Angeles, where Taylor finally diffused it, deploying her famous raunchiness. As Pendleton tells it, Taylor had been drinking; she had just learned that her friend Anwar Sadat, the Egyptian president, had been assassinated. Hellman, also drunk, initially offered Taylor her sympathy. But later, when she carped about the real-life models for her characters, Taylor told her to knock it off. Hellman refused, calling Taylor "Miss Lizzie" to provoke a fight.

Taylor was silent. Observers wondered what she would

do. She looked Hellman in the eye. "You can call me cunt," she said slowly. "But do not call me Miss Lizzie."

Taylor prospered as Regina—in a way denied her as a Washington wife. Order had returned to the universe: Taylor was again a star. This magnified her differences with Warner. After Reagan was shot, Pendleton said, Taylor proposed putting a full-page ad for gun control in the *Washington Post* and the *New York Times*. But Warner dissuaded her—winning a battle but losing the war. Soon thereafter, the marriage was over.

In 1982, *The Little Foxes* moved to London, where, conveniently, Burton had just divorced Suzy Hunt. Pendleton will never forget Taylor and Burton's public reunion: "I'm standing at the bar with these character actors—these grizzled veterans of the stage. Nothing gets to them. And all of a sudden—outside—we see flashbulbs. In the door walks Elizabeth Taylor on the arm of Richard Burton." The grizzled actors grew misty-eyed. "It was so touching, so moving. They looked so beautiful together."

18

1982–1984

FOR THIS BOOK to have an old-fashioned Hollywood ending, I would have to stop here—with the Burtons reunited, more blindingly luminous than all the flashbulbs exploding around them. Taylor is incandescent: her ability as a stage actress finally recognized, her beauty restored, in the company of a light source as powerful as her own. Joy is frozen in this moment, along with fidelity. The moment shouts: happily ever after.

But Taylor's best movies don't end that way, so neither will this book. Velvet's victory is tinged with loss; she fell off the horse. Angela said good-bye to George on death row, and Gloria—brave Gloria, who dared to assert ownership of her own body—was punished for this with death. Leslie was no stranger to grief: the Mexican baby whom she saved was killed in World War II. Catherine left the state asylum with her brain intact but her family in shambles. The minister who taught Laura to trust could not remain with her. And Martha—frightened Martha, cowering against the dawn—likely slept off her hangover and tormented yet more junior faculty after dark.

Screenplays can be quirky, but they adhere to certain conventions. They focus on a hero who desires something, but who must defeat an enemy to obtain it. The enemy can be as concrete as another person or as abstract as the natural world. Often the enemy is an aspect of the hero herself—a cunning adversary who undermines from within. Sometimes she has many enemies. There is only rule: by the end of act 2, the enemies must be ahead. They must seem impossible to defeat. To battle them, the hero has to face her deepest fears.

In a screenplay of Taylor's life, her glittering reunion with Burton—set against the backdrop of her fiftieth birthday party—would occur in act 2. It would be suffused with hope. Yet something would foreshadow trouble—an incident as small as, say, the cavalier way that Burton treated Taylor's director when they were first introduced. Pendleton, who did not take offense, recalled: "Richard Burton looked at me. He did not say hello. He did not say anything. He said, 'She does one fucking play, she thinks she's Eleanora Duse.'"

Taylor seemed to enjoy the put-down. Aglow in their shared celebrity, the Burtons swapped insults for hours, as if their second divorce had never happened. They left together, conspicuously, at the height of the party. Pendleton didn't speak with Taylor until a few nights later, when he went to her dressing room to give her notes on her performance. She shut the door behind him. "'I have to talk to you,' she said. I thought she would bring up something about the show," Pendleton recalled. "But then she said, 'Should I marry Richard again?'" Pendleton was speechless. "Remember, I'm from Warren, Ohio. I can't believe Elizabeth Taylor is asking me this.

"Has he suggested that?" Pendleton replied. "And she said, 'Yes, he was over at the house a couple nights ago—we were in the kitchen—and he said, 'Will you marry me again?' " Pendleton paused. "I had no idea what to say, but when you're with her you don't feel there's a right answer or a wrong answer. So I finally said, 'Do you want to?' And she said, 'I don't know.' " The issue wasn't Burton. The issue was marriage: "Should we try *that* again?"

For a while, Burton appeared to have become a better man—a supportive one, even. After seeing *The Little Foxes*, he dropped all his snide comparisons to Duse. Backstage following the show, he looked "openly astonished," the cast members recalled. "And humbled."

But Taylor and he did not remarry. Perhaps his drinking scared her. By 1981, his liver and kidneys were already cirrhotic. Or perhaps she was unnerved by his other addiction—to young women—which Richard McWhorter delicately described this way: "He had an eye."

Burton's "eye" propelled Taylor closer to the climax of her personal act 2. In 1983, she agreed to star opposite him in a production of Noël Coward's *Private Lives*. It played to full houses on Broadway and on the road. It earned them millions. But during its run, Burton married Sally Hay, a freelance production assistant. And Taylor took up with her old friend, Jack Daniel's. "I never touched a drop before the show," Taylor confessed in her 1987 book. "I was too professional for that, but the minute the curtain went down, Jack Daniel's was waiting in the wings." As was Demerol.

The play deals with Amanda and Elyot—a divorced

couple—who reunite after meeting by accident while on honeymoons with their new spouses. Amanda and Elyot have an irresistible, yet destructive bond—similar to the one that had existed between Taylor and Burton. But by 1983, the real-life stars seemed linked by little more than mutual rancor—so ponderous that it sucked the air out of Coward's soufflé. This production has "all the vitality of a Madame Tussaud's exhibit and the gaiety of a tax audit," Frank Rich wrote in the *New York Times*. Worse, Rich said, it belied the promise that Taylor had shown in *The Little Foxes*.

The run ended on November 6, 1983. Taylor returned to Los Angeles, where, thanks to Jack Daniel's and Demerol, she began passing out with her eyes open. After one such frightening episode, her children and close friends confronted her in her room at Cedars-Sinai Hospital. They forced her to look at what she was doing to herself. It was, Taylor wrote in her memoir, a classic "family intervention." On December 5, 1983, Taylor checked into the Betty Ford Center in Rancho Mirage, California. In her first harrowing week, she banished toxins from her body. For the rest of her stay, she began to feel again, and to deal with what she felt.

"The entire process of tearing down and rebuilding on a solid foundation of self-awareness makes it possible for almost anyone to conquer those demons," Taylor wrote.

If one has to feel and see after a long period of anesthesia, the Bel Air house to which Taylor returned was an excellent place to do this. Located at the top of Nimes Road, it has an Olympian quality. Its air was purer, clearer, above the orange haze below.

At 7,100 square feet, the house occupied only a small patch of its 1.27-acre lot—a cabin, by Bel Air standards. Taylor let the trees around it grow thick. They blocked a striking view of downtown Los Angeles for something more important: privacy. If she couldn't see out, the paparazzi couldn't see in.

Lush, well-tended gardens also insulated the house. Succulents grew from a retaining wall around the driveway, softening its appearance. Her backyard exploded with foxgloves, snapdragons, hydrangeas, and lamb's ears—plants she would have encountered during her English childhood. It also held a greenhouse, in whose heavy air, tender orchids pushed up shoots. Farther back, amid a jungle of towering bamboo, was a secluded picnic table—a secret, exotic spot.

Considering Taylor's resources, the house was jaw-droppingly unpretentious—a cozy buffer against the roughness of the outside world. Shag carpeting covered every floor. Silk-upholstered walls absorbed jarring sounds. It wasn't a hard-edged, midcentury modern house, like the home she occupied in Benedict Canyon. It was a ranch-style house, built by Nancy Sinatra Sr., in 1960. The jewels and paintings Taylor stored in it, however, were far from commonplace—warranting high-tech security and Israeli-trained guards.

Some of her art had comforting associations. Her Frans Hals portrait and Pissarro landscape once brightened her room at Harkness Memorial Pavilion—a gift from Mike Todd during her 1957 back surgery. Other pieces recalled more chaotic times.

In her life before sobriety, Taylor had palled around with Andy Warhol's circle, occasionally surfacing at Studio 54. But Bob Colacello, founding editor of Warhol's *Interview*, told me that she had cooled somewhat toward him after he detailed her antics in *Holy Terror: Andy Warhol Close Up*. These antics included downing a "Debauched Mary" ("five parts vodka and one part blood") after arriving six hours late to the set of *The Driver's Seat*, and, after appearing two hours late at a luncheon in her honor, demanding multiple bourbons and obsessively plucking leaves from a hedge and piling them on a table. He also mentioned a New York party at which she puffed on "big fat joints of Brazilian marijuana" before "aiming chocolate-covered strawberries at passing pedestrians." Yet whatever irritation she may have felt with Warhol's crowd, she appreciated his art. His iconic silkscreen portrait of her dominated her living room.

Taylor's modest kitchen, with its wicker chairs and Mickey Mouse clock, made me think of something that Liz Smith had said: "No movie of hers quite captures the rather ordinary woman she is—full of fun, rather wacky, often wise, often foolish, her life and her motivations inevitably morphed by fame. When you are with her, it is her history and the atmosphere around her that are daunting. She is just a short, funny gal who wants to talk about what's next on the menu."

I could picture that gal in this house, sinking her toes into the carpet, dangling her feet in the swimming pool, whose lining twinkles with iridescent tiles. (Christopher Taylor, son of her brother Howard, did the mosaic work.) I could picture her in her upstairs bedroom—an octagonal space with big windows and a wraparound balcony that felt breezy—kookie—like a tree house or Laura Reynolds's beatnik pad in *The Sandpiper.*

Taylor loved looking down on the garden from her bedroom. One tree in particular inspired her. "Its three roots were twined around each other and then bent over to hug the ground," she wrote in her memoir. "I think tree surgeons use the term 'tortured.'" Yet it endured, renewing itself each spring. "Anytime I've wanted to give in to the dark forces in my life—from over-eating to self-pity—I look at that tree and find the courage to go on."

In her house, beside that tree, Taylor chose a path to which "accidental" no longer applied. This path required bravery. She had taken challenging paths before—when, for example, she overcame Vatican opposition to adopt Maria Burton. But the obstacles on her new path were larger. In Los Angeles and elsewhere, she saw gay men, including her beloved *Giant* costar, Rock Hudson, wasting from an illness that could be neither treated nor cured. Worse, heterosexuals in the entertainment industry, who had once made money from the talents of these gay men, now shunned them.

Taylor was not one to desert her friends. "She has been surrounded by gay men who doted on her, her entire life," Liz Smith said in 2009. "And a great many of her friendships—

gay or straight—spring from her wanting to help a bird with a wing down."

So she stepped up, changing with one decision the way the world remembers her. No director told her to do this. No booze affected her choice. "It was," Kate Burton said, "her greatest conscious gift."

19

Her Greatest Conscious Gift, 1984–2011

You are not here. You are nowhere.
Your son is dying upstairs, right above your head.
You can do nothing.
You can do nothing.
You can do nothing.

—Brenda Freiberg, "A Secret Gift," 2008
(Freiberg's two sons both died of AIDS)

It's bad enough that people are dying of AIDS, but no one should die of ignorance. —Elizabeth Taylor testifying before the Labor, Health and Human Services Senate Subcommittee, May 8, 1986

WHEN I LOOK BACK on the last decades of Taylor's life, I cannot help but think of Virginia Woolf—not just Taylor's 1966 movie but the writer to whom its title alludes.

In *Three Guineas*, Woolf set down some goals and guidelines for women, which, although they were written in 1938, jibe uncannily with the goals and guidelines of third-wave feminism, formulated more than fifty years later. They also jibe with how Elizabeth Taylor intuitively lived her life.

Woolf urged women to question patriarchal authority—to ridicule its trappings. "A woman who advertised her motherhood by a tuft of horsehair on the left shoulder would scarcely, you will agree, be a venerable object," she wrote. Woolf told them not to mistake formal education (from which their mothers had been excluded) for wisdom. And even if they gained access to institutions previously closed to women, they should stand apart, in a Society of Outsiders, daring to oppose the majority for justice's sake.

In 1985, when Taylor joined the fight against AIDS, she entered into a true Society of Outsiders. It was more inclusive than the one Woolf proposed—containing men as well as women. But its goals—and its adversarial relationship to the majority—were similar.

The 1980s were a harsh, smug decade. In 1979, Jerry Falwell, a Southern Baptist minister in Lynchburg, Virginia, founded the Moral Majority, an extremist organization that used religion as a pretext to scare average people and whip up antipluralism. Without Falwell's showboating, AIDS would have been just another epidemic: a medical problem, not a political one. But in the illness he saw an opportunity to foment hate. In 1983, on his TV show, *Old Time Gospel Hour*, he called AIDS "the judgment of God upon moral perversion in this society."

Falwell had no patience with Christian charity or forgiveness. His group was a political entity, part of the powerful

New Right, to which President Ronald Reagan felt he owed his landslide victory in 1980. This allegiance colored the U.S. government's handling of the epidemic. Because AIDS seemed only to affect marginal communities—homosexuals, hemophiliacs, and intravenous-drug users—the Reagan administration ignored it. Even within the academic medical community, the disease was viewed as a scary, controversial puzzle.

In January 1981, Dr. Michael Gottlieb, then a thirty-three-year-old immunologist working on experimental transplants at UCLA, saw his first AIDS patient: a gaunt youth, ravaged by an opportunistic infection, his immune system shot. In the next five months he saw four more. Concerned that the pattern might have public-health consequences, on June 5, 1981, he made a nine-paragraph report to the U.S. Centers for Disease Control, identifying AIDS. He followed this report with a peer-reviewed paper on AIDS in the *New England Journal of Medicine* on December 10. For people in Los Angeles with HIV, Gottlieb became the man to see. Rock Hudson was his patient.

Like other physicians at the beginning of the epidemic, Gottlieb often felt helpless. "We were young doctors with young patients who were *dying*," he said. "They had the disease; we had the frustration of not knowing how to treat them. We could offer very little, other than our sincere efforts—and hand-holding."

To treat AIDS patients, doctors had to "make common cause with the sick," Gottlieb said, using a phrase coined by physician and global health activist Paul Farmer. Many of the doctors, including Gottlieb himself, were conventional heterosexual men. But to serve their patients, they had to align themselves with those hardest hit: gay men. They had to join with society's outsiders.

The need to do this divided the medical community. As a medical student in 1982, Dr. Francine Hanberg, now an infectious-disease specialist who treats people with HIV, saw her first AIDS patient. He had been flown by helicopter from California's Central Valley to Stanford University Medical Center, where he was pronounced dead on arrival. Hanberg vividly remembers both the patient—and the annoyance that he caused to some of the emergency room staff. "Why did they bring him to us?" one colleague grumbled, irritated at having to deal with the body.

"Because he's twenty-five years old!" Hanberg replied, livid. "Because it's a new, mysterious disease. It's going to be big. And they were hoping we could do something for him."

Hanberg was right about its magnitude. By 1985, 15,527 AIDS cases had been confirmed in fifty-one countries. All but three thousand of those cases had resulted in death; the rest were expected to follow. These numbers mocked the U.S. government's initial stinting response.

During the epidemic's first year—June 1981 to June 1982—the U.S. Centers for Disease Control and Prevention (CDC) spent only $1 million on AIDS, as opposed to $9 million on a far slighter problem, Legionnaires' disease. In 1982, Congress allocated $2.6 million for the CDC's AIDS research, but the White House opposed the allocation and tried to block future spending on research and prevention.

Although Democrats held a majority in Congress, representatives from areas worst hit by the crisis—New York City, San Francisco, and Los Angeles—faced two ongoing battles: one, of course, for money; the other for a recognition of the situation's gravity. Reagan never even uttered the word "AIDS" in a speech until 1987, when, on the eve of the *Third* International AIDS Conference in Washington, D.C., he could no longer shrug off a global epidemic.

Without private fund-raising, AIDS research and education would have stalled in the epidemic's critical first years. And without Elizabeth Taylor leading the charge, private fund-raising would likely have stalled, too.

"I don't think anyone else could have done it," Gottlieb said. "No one else had the strength, the celebrity, and the will to do it.

"Someone in a leadership position—a president or a first lady—could have told the country: 'Do the right thing,'" Gottlieb continued. And the country would have listened. But no one in power rose to the moral occasion.

The cause needed "a woman at the pinnacle," he explained. "Because openly gay men are not given the respect that they are due. And if a straight man speaks up on a gay issue, his orientation becomes suspect. Elizabeth was perfect for the role. And I think she knew that."

The year 1984 was tough for Taylor. On August 5, Richard Burton died suddenly of a brain hemorrhage at his home in Switzerland. He and Taylor had made peace since their scorched-earth tour in *Private Lives*, and she had hoped to attend his funeral. But his widow, Sally Hay, made clear that Taylor was not welcome.

Things did not improve in 1985. On July 15, a rail-thin Rock Hudson made his last public appearance—to help Doris Day promote a new TV show. He then flew from L.A. to Paris for an experimental AIDS treatment, which he was too weak to receive. After returning to L.A. on a private flight, he was airlifted to UCLA Medical Center, where, on July 25, he gave Gottlieb permission to go public with his diagnosis. Gottlieb's brief announcement stunned mainstream Americans. They felt as if they had known Hudson; he had been inside their own living rooms—as a star of *Dynasty* and *McMillan & Wife*. Some began to realize: AIDS wasn't just a disease of "those people."

In 12-step recovery programs, addicts learn to help themselves by reaching out to others. In 1985, when Taylor lent her name to AIDS Project Los Angeles (APLA), she believed that she was doing this—honoring Hudson by reaching out to strangers—far beyond her immediate circle. But the disease soon struck her immediate family. Taylor's daughter-in-law, Aileen Getty, then married to Christopher Wilding, learned that she was HIV positive, a consequence of an unsafe affair.

Taylor threw herself into recruiting luminaries for the first APLA "Commitment to Life" dinner, an ambitious fundraiser set for September 19 at Los Angeles's Bonaventure Hotel. Its guest of honor was Betty Ford, to whose treatment center she owed her sobriety. But her friends did not leap to help. Many hung up on her. Frank Sinatra called AIDS another of her "lame-dog causes." She received anonymous death threats. Yet she soldiered on, recruiting, among others, Sammy Davis Jr., Rod Stewart, Stevie Wonder, and Cher to attend. The dinner raised $1.3 million—more money in one night than the CDC had spent on the epidemic in its entire first year.

That night she also found something she had not thought existed: a use for her celebrity. A reason for enduring metaphorically what her *Suddenly, Last Summer* character had experienced literally: standing on a catwalk above a crazy mob, its fingers grabbing ceaselessly at her ankles.

"When I saw that my fame could help in my fight against AIDS, I thought, Bring it on!" she told Liz Smith. "If people wanted to come to an AIDS event to see whether I was fat or thin, pretty or not, or really had violet eyes, then great, just come. My fame finally made sense to me."

She did not stop with APLA. Later that year, with Gottlieb and Dr. Mathilde Krim, a New York–based cancer researcher who had set up the AIDS Medical Foundation, Taylor helped start the American Foundation for AIDS Research (AmfAR)—now the foremost national nonprofit devoted to AIDS research and prevention.

Her courage fortified people with HIV. It worked synergistically with the new medications—the protease inhibitors and the reverse transcriptase inhibitors—that by the 1990s had begun to emerge from labs which AmfAR had helped to fund. "At a time when the disgust, neglect, and derision of the broader society and culture was making people with AIDS feel dirty and ashamed, Elizabeth Taylor blessed us with her glamour," AIDS activist Sean Strub wrote after her death.

On September 20, 1986, APLA honored Taylor at its second "Commitment to Life" event, which had evolved from a dinner into a show at the Wiltern Theater. Produced by Hollywood agent Barry Krost, the show filled the giant venue—with Madonna, Billy Crystal, Cyndi Lauper, Bruce Willis, and nearly every iconic 1980s face either on the stage or in the audience. There were inexpensive seats, too—to include regular people who wanted to contribute to the cause.

Like most award booklets, the "Commitment to Life" programs contain tributes from friends and associates of the honoree. Not surprisingly, Taylor's booklet was very thick—she had lots of friends. I was amazed, however, at who was among them: Nancy Reagan—whose husband's willful ignorance had created many of the obstacles Taylor was struggling to overcome.

When Taylor accepted the award, she vowed to spend the rest of her life fighting AIDS, which she did. In 1990, she testified before Congress in support of the Ryan White Comprehensive AIDS Resources Emergency Care Act, which passed in August of that year. In 1991, she created the Elizabeth Taylor AIDS Foundation, not for research but to assist people living with HIV. In its first decade, the foundation raised more than $50 million.

No vaccine yet exists for AIDS, though scientists continue to search for one. In the 1980s, French virologist Luc Montagnier (who identified the AIDS retrovirus) and U.S. researcher Robert Gallo (who devised a test to diagnose the

HIV infection) made the first big breakthroughs. In 1996, Dr. David Ho, founding director of the Aaron Diamond AIDS Research Center in New York City, is credited with the next major advance: a "cocktail" of protease inhibitors and reverse transcriptase inhibitors that would permit a person with HIV to survive without developing AIDS. Ho met Taylor in the 1980s, when he was a medical resident at Cedars-Sinai in Los Angeles. To him, her greatest achievement was not the money that she raised but the way she helped overcome the stigma surrounding AIDS. "On a personal level, she did a great deal to bring public attention to the disease," he told me.

Taylor's intuitive grasp of Virginia Woolf's guidelines for women did not extend to an embrace of poverty. Woolf insisted that women support themselves, but urged them to do their jobs for "love of the work itself" when they had enough to live on. Taylor had no reservations about making money—launching her multiscent perfume empire in 1988 and the House of Taylor, a jewelry maker and distributor, in 2005. At her death, the press estimated her net worth to be between $600 million and $1 billion. (A Taylor spokesperson, however, characterized those estimates as "wildly exaggerated.")

Taylor also worked hard to maintain her sobriety. In 1988, she returned to the Betty Ford Center, leaving with a new best friend, Larry Fortensky, a handsome construction worker who, she said, made her laugh. Three years later, she married Fortensky at Neverland, the California ranch owned by another best friend, the late pop singer Michael Jackson, who underwrote the $2-million celebration.

Ever loyal to her friends, Taylor stood by Jackson in 1993 when he was accused of child molestation. They were linked, she said, by their "horrible childhoods." "Working at the age of nine is not a childhood," she told talk show host Larry King. "He started at the age of three." When Jackson was again charged in 2003, she continued to defend him—suggesting that his wealth might have made him a target for people seeking a payoff. "I've never been so angry in my life," she said about the allegation.

On June 25, 2009, Jackson died unexpectedly at age fifty. "I really was concerned about her," Kate Burton said, "because I know how close they were." Prudently, Taylor avoided his circuslike public memorial at the Staples Center in L.A. So many fans wanted tickets that they had to be dispensed via lottery.

I had hoped to speak with Taylor about feminism, regardless of what she would say. Kate Burton saw the thread of feminism in some of her stepmother's movies but doubted Taylor had been conscious of it. "I don't see her thinking of herself as a feminist," Burton said. "I think she just does what she does."

The people around Taylor told me her health was too frail for an interview. Many thought my project might amuse her—though no one would say this for attribution. I assumed her fragility was made up, an excuse not to talk. But on March 23, 2011, when she died of congestive heart failure in Cedars-Sinai Hospital, I realized they had told me the truth.

Her death was met with an outpouring of grief and love. And hate: The Westboro Baptist Church—carrying Falwell's torch of bigotry—threatened to picket her funeral. Margie Phelps, daughter of Fred Phelps, the group's leader, fired off multiple attacks via Twitter, including this one: "No RIP Elizabeth Taylor who spent her life in adultery and enabling proud fags."

Taylor's small service at Forest Lawn Memorial Park, however, thwarted the protesters. It was limited to fewer than one hundred close friends and family. In death as in life, she mocked herself—arranging for her remains to arrive at the mausoleum fifteen minutes late.

As columnist Katha Pollitt observed, "Feminism is a social justice movement." From 1985 until her death, Taylor fought consciously—not accidentally—for social justice. I believe her final role in life was influenced by the movies with feminist content that she had starred in as a younger woman. Actors both shape and are shaped by their parts. They bring aspects of themselves to their characters, and they take aspects of their characters away.

Two parts that Taylor played for director George Stevens seem to have had a strong effect on her identity in later life. Stevens saw qualities in her as a teenager that she had not yet recognized in herself. He saw the qualities that would enable her to make "her greatest conscious gift."

When Stevens ad-libbed the "Tell Mama" line for her in *A Place in the Sun*, he identified a maternal quality in her love. This quality, journalist Kevin Sessums wrote, also informed her AIDS activism. In a memorial tribute published in the *Daily Beast*, Sessums described an interview that he had with her in the 1990s for *POZ*, a magazine for people with HIV. He told Taylor that he felt she had turned to "all of us who were HIV positive" and said, "Tell Mama—"

Taylor stopped him and touched his hand, he recalled. Then, as if to confirm his perception, she finished the line herself: "Tell Mama all."

Taylor's character in *Giant* also anticipated the activist she would become. As Leslie Benedict, Taylor makes common cause with the sick. She steps away from her privileged community—the white Texas ranching elite—to serve a community of outsiders, their Mexican workers. Although she is warned not to enter the Mexican homes, she does so anyway. And when she finds an ailing child, she cradles him. She doesn't pull back, fearing contagion—just as Taylor herself did not recoil from people with HIV. She demands medical attention from the privileged community's physician.

Her husband scolds her. "He's *our* doctor," he says. "He don't tend those people."

Although frustrated, Leslie holds her temper. Decrying his prejudice would not help the child. Gently, through persuasion, she forces both her husband and the doctor to transcend their bigotry: to acknowledge the humanity—and the suffering—of the outsiders.

"Darling, I don't think you quite understand," Leslie says sweetly. "There's a child who's very sick." Then she turns to the physician: "You'll go, won't you doctor?"

And in that brave moment, Leslie leads the doctor—as Taylor herself led a callous nation—to do the right thing.

Acknowledgments

I did not watch Elizabeth Taylor's movies alone in the dark. I watched them many times with different friends, all of whom offered valuable insight. Robin Swicord and Nick Kazan inadvertently got the project rolling—by giving me a boxed set of Taylor DVDs. Robin repeatedly weathered *Cleopatra* with me, as well as commented on my drafts.

The movies I highlight are a pleasure to watch. Not all Taylor's movies, however, can be described this way. Thanks to Robert Ladendorf for enduring many less-than-beguiling films with me. Robert also tracked down Production Code memos in the Academy of Motion Picture Arts and Sciences Margaret Herrick Library and gave me thoughtful notes on my every draft. (At last a use for that master's in film!) In the Herrick Library Special Collections, thanks to Barbara Hall, research archivist, and Jenny Romero, coordinator. Thanks also to Faye Thompson, coordinator of the Herrick Library's Roddy McDowall Photo Archive. I also benefited from the assistance of Robert Montoya in the Department of Special Collections in the Charles E. Young Research Library at

UCLA and Susan Halpert at the Houghton Library at Harvard University.

For their careful readings of the manuscript, thanks to Sarah Kroll-Rosenbaum, Brighde Mullins, and Ellen Handler Spitz. For Memorial Day in Palm Springs, thanks to Hayes Michel. For joining me in study hall, thanks to Nan Cohen, Tim Kirkman, and Tom Rastrelli. For their perspective on *Giant*, thanks to Lindsay Doran and Rodney Kemerer. Thanks to Jonathan and Rita Lynn for introducing me to Austin Pendleton, who was generous with his time and wit. Thanks to David Francis, Judith Freeman, and Marion Rosenberg for an intriguing off-the-record conversation. For recollections of the early days of the AIDS epidemic, thank you to Dr. Michael Gottlieb, Dr. Francine Hanberg, Brenda Freiberg, and Barry Krost. Thanks to Kathy Lu for introducing me to Dr. David Ho.

Thank you to Dinah Lenney for introducing me to Kate Burton, and to Kate for allowing me a glimpse of the person beneath Taylor's public identity. I benefited from conversations with these old and new friends: Marlene Beggelman, Johanna Blakley, Donna Bojarsky, Jon Boorstin, Dorothy Braudy, Leo Braudy, Natasha Burton, Kate Chilton, Meg Cimino, Donna Deitch, Sara Epstein, Nancy Furlotti, Vivian Gornick, James Grissom, Libby Halstead, Anthony Hernandez, Margo Howard, Terri Jentz, Laura Karpman, Zoe Kazan, Jeffrey Kegler, Fran Kiernan, Howard Kiernan, Cheris Kramarae, Nora Kroll-Rosenbaum, Adam Kurtzman, Caryn Leland, Tom Lutz, Kate McCarthy, Vance Muse, William Nguyen, Sarah Conley Odenkirk, Jere Pfister, Owen Phillips,

Laurie Pike, Claire Potter, John Romano, Nancy Romano, Kevin Sessums, Victoria Steele, Arne Svensen, Susan Brodsky Thalken, Shelley Wanger, Laurie Winer, and Jaime Wolf. I'm also grateful to family: Mike Lord, Nancy McWhorter Lord, and Richard McWhorter. Thank you to Adele Cygelman, David Mossler, and Brenda Potter for admitting me to houses where Taylor once lived. As always, thanks to Mary Lamont, my stalwart transcriber.

This book benefited greatly from the stewardship of two feminist men: George Gibson, my deft and insightful editor, and Eric Simonoff, my shrewd and steadfast agent. I am also grateful to Patti Ratchford for the knock-out jacket, Vicki Haire for creating the illusion that I can spell, and Mike O'Connor, for his attention to detail. Without Shannon Halwes, there would be no book. Not only did she read every draft and share her knowledge of movies, she feigned convincing enthusiasm when I insisted that we watch *Who's Afraid of Virgina Woolf?* for a fourteenth time.

Notes

1. The Beautiful Somnambulist

1 "I myself have never . . .": Rebecca West, "Mr. Chesterton in Hysterics," reprinted in *The Young Rebecca: The Writings of Rebecca West, 1911–17*, ed. Jane Marcus (New York: Virago Press, 1982), 219.

2 "a movement to end sexism . . .": bell hooks, *Feminism is for Everybody: Passionate Politics* (London: Pluto Press, 2000), 1.

2 "the radical notion that women . . .": Marie Shear, "Media Watch: Celebrating Women's Words," *New Directions for Women*, May/June 1986, 6. Often attributed to Cheris Kramarae and Paula Treichler, the quote actually comes from Marie Shear. Kramarae asked Shear for the origin of the quote, and Shear explained, "I've been calling feminism 'the radical notion that women are people' since God was a child." But when Shear used the definition in a 1986 review of *A Feminist Dictionary* in *New Directions for Women*, the definition "reached thousands of readers." Shear adds: "The idea

certainly isn't uniquely mine. For example, Rosalie Maggio's trove, *The New Beacon Book of Quotations by Women*, quotes Katha Pollitt thusly: 'For me, to be a feminist is to answer the question "Are women human?" with a yes.' "

2 "a social justice movement . . .": Katha Pollitt in "Rebecca Traister, Hanna Rosin, and Others on Why You Can't Own Feminism," *Slate*, October 8, 2010, http://www.slate.com/id/2270053/entry/2270054.

2 "is to integrate an ideology . . .": Rebecca Walker, "Becoming the Third Wave," *Ms.*, January/February 1992, 41.

3 Camille Paglia: Camille Paglia, "Elizabeth Taylor: Hollywood's Pagan Queen," *Penthouse*, March 1992, reprinted in *Sex, Art, and American Culture* (New York: Vintage Books, 1992).

5 "Mothers were said . . .": Barbara G. Walker, *The Skeptical Feminist: Discovering the Virgin, Mother, and Crone* (San Francisco: Harper & Row, 1987), 12.

7 "an aura of heightened reality": Walker Percy, *The Moviegoer* (New York: Ballantine Books, 1990), 13.

7 "a kind of possessiveness . . .": Leo Braudy, *The Frenzy of Renown: Fame and Its History* (New York: Vintage Books, 1997), 606.

7 "Elizabeth was very devoted to her mother . . .": Interview with Kate Burton, New York City, May 14, 2010. (All Burton quotations are from this interview.)

8 "Bust Inspectors": Ellis Amburn, *The Most Beautiful Woman in the World: The Obsessions, Passions and Courage of Elizabeth Taylor* (New York: HarperCollins, 2000), 12.

8 "If the cameraman . . .": Ibid., 11.

8 Brenda Maddox: Brenda Maddox, *Who's Afraid of Elizabeth Taylor?* (New York: M. Evans, 1977).

9 "Elizabeth did something when it required . . .": Elton John, quoted in Brad Goldfarb, "Talking to Elton John," *Interview*, February 2007, 207.

9 "This is what forty looks like": Elizabeth Taylor, *Elizabeth Takes Off: On Weight Gain, Weight Loss, Self-Image, and Self-Esteem* (New York: Putnam, 1987), 26.

10 Katharine Hepburn's sexuality is detailed in William J. Mann, *Kate: The Woman Who Was Hepburn* (New York: Henry Holt, 2006).

10 "erotic vagrancy": Quoted in Liz Smith, "Liz Taylor Returning to Stage," *New York Post*, August 23, 2007.

10 "Can I sue the Pope?": Ibid.

11 "All profoundly original art looks ugly at first": Clement Greenberg, "Art," *The Nation*, April 7, 1945, 397–98.

2. *National Velvet*, 1944

14 "clubs to which her own sex . . .": Virginia Woolf, *Three Guineas* (New York: Harcourt Brace, 1938), 85.

14 "colleges from which . . .": Ibid.

14 "racecourses where she . . .": Ibid.

15 Handmade birthday cards and Valentines to Clarence Brown: C. David Heymann, *Liz: An Intimate Biography of Elizabeth Taylor* (New York: Birch Lane Press, 1995), 41–43.

16 "like the rumps of elephants . . .": Enid Bagnold, *National Velvet* (New York: HarperFestival, 2002), 3.

18 "thin as famine": Ibid.,131.

20 "emotional intelligence": Daniel Goleman, *Emotional Intelligence: Why It Can Matter More Than IQ* (New York: Bantam Books, 1996).

22 "Mummie's" toilet: Elizabeth Taylor, *Nibbles and Me* (New York: Simon & Schuster Children's Publishing, 2002), 19–21.

22 "I knew he would . . .": Ibid., 12.

3. 1945–1950

23 "the most beautiful creature . . .": J. D. Salinger, quoted in Kitty Kelley, *Elizabeth Taylor: The Last Star* (New York: Simon & Schuster, 2001), 19.

24 "The novel is about female ambition": Interview with Robin Swicord, Los Angeles, November 18, 2009.

25 Relationship of Adrian and Francis Taylor: Heymann, *Liz*, 60.

25 "Janet's husband . . .": Diana McLellan, *The Girls: Sappho Goes to Hollywood* (New York: St. Martin's Press, 2000), 260.

25 Sara Taylor's affair with Michael Curtiz: Amburn, *The Most Beautiful Woman in the World*, 9.

27 "dream girl," every man's ideal: George Stevens to William Miklejohn, memo, May 42, 1949, George Stevens Archive, Margaret Herrick Library, Academy of Motion Picture Arts and Sciences (hereafter cited as AMPAS).

28 "Angela is not bound by the need . . .": George Stevens, "The Role of Angela Vickers," undated memo, in ibid.

28 "spoil and limit the world . . .": Ibid.

28 Taylor . . . understood little beyond the price of a cashmere sweater: Kelley, *Elizabeth Taylor,* 37.

28 "Elizabeth Taylor is a joy to watch . . .": Hollis Alpert, "A Double Bounty from Hollywood," *Saturday Review of Literature,* September 1, 1951, 28–31.

29 "boldest scene . . .": "Cinema: The New Pictures," *Time,* September 10, 1951. http://www.time.com/time/magazine/article/0,9171,815385,00.html.

4. *A Place in the Sun,* 1951

30 "Your problem is this . . .": Michael Wilson, "A Place in the Sun," First Change Draft, November 23, 1949, 65, Michael Wilson Archive, Charles E. Young Research Library, UCLA.

30 "You understand . . .": "History of Cinema Series: Hollywood and the Production Code," Department of Special Collections, Margaret Herrick Library, AMPAS.

31 Louis B. Mayer: Neal Gabler, *An Empire of Their Own: How the Jews Invented Hollywood* (New York: Anchor Books, 1989).

32 "These Jews seem . . .": Joseph I. Breen, quoted in Thomas Doherty, *Hollywood's Censor: Joseph I. Breen and the Production Code Administration* (New York: Columbia University Press, 2007), 199.

32 "eccentric utterances . . .": Ibid.

33 The Production Code and amendments to it: Ibid., 351–63.

34 "Please omit the action . . .": Joseph I. Breen to Louis B. Mayer, letter, February 11, 1943, "History of Cinema Series:

Hollywood and the Production Code," reel 27, Production Code Archive, Margaret Herrick Library, AMPAS.

36 "We feel this story . . .": Joseph I. Breen to Luigi Luraschi, letter, September 30, 1949, in ibid.

36 "George's line, 'I'll think of something' . . .": Ibid.

36 "Please rewrite . . .": Ibid.

36 "Please omit the following dialog . . ." Ibid.

37 "The players, barely visible . . .": "Cinema: The New Pictures," *Time*, September 10, 1951, http://www.time.com/time/magazine/article/0,9171,815385,00.html.

5. 1951–1955

39 Stevens directing Taylor is detailed in William Mann, *How to Be a Movie Star: Elizabeth Taylor in Hollywood* (Boston: Houghon Mifflin Harcourt, 2009), 102

40 "Nick's every bit as dynamic . . .": Hedda Hopper, "When a Girl Marries," *Modern Screen*, November 1956, 96.

40 Musical version of *An American Tragedy:* Hedda Hopper, "Crosby, Hendrix to do 'Tragedy' with Music," *Los Angeles Times*, March 22, 1949.

41 "It must be those huge breasts of hers . . .": Maria Riva, *Marlene Dietrich* (New York: Ballantine Books, 1994), 626.

41 "should never have been made by me . . .": Elizabeth Taylor, quoted in Randy Taraborelli, *Elizabeth (*New York: Warner Books, 2006), 113.

43 Hudson chooses Taylor for *Giant*: Amburn, *The Most Beautiful Woman in the World*, 61.

6. *Giant*, 1956

44 "bringing back many people . . .": "SINDLINGER FINDS MOVIE GROWTH SPARKED BY SUCCESS OF GIANT," press release from Albert Sindlinger Associates, Ridley Park, Pennsylvania, March 1, 1956, George Stevens Archive, Margaret Herrick Library, AMPAS.

45 "There they found . . .": Sara Evans, *Personal Politics: The Roots of Women's Liberation in the Civil Rights Movement and the New Left* (New York: Vintage, 1980), 23.

48 "Reading Giant . . .": Jonathan Yardley, "Ferber's 'Giant' Cut Down to Size," *Washington Post*, May 8, 2006, http://www.washingtonpost.com/wp-dyn/content/article/2006/05/07/AR2006050701112.html.

52 "depicts the erosion . . .": Peter Biskind, *Seeing Is Believing: How Hollywood Taught Us to Stop Worrying and Love the Fifties* (New York: Pantheon Books, 1983).

53 "aggregate of pluralist values . . .": Ibid., 293.

7. 1956–1959

54 "Bick Benedict . . .": Copy of ad in *Giant* publicity file, George Stevens Archive, Margaret Herrick Library, AMPAS. (All quotations from this ad are in the same file.)

55 "the extreme mental duress . . .": Dr. John H. Davis to A. Morgan Maree, letter re: "Elizabeth Wilding," March 12, 1956, George Stevens Archive, Department of Special Collections, Margaret Herrick Library, AMPAS.

57 Clift's drinking: Patricia Bosworth, *Montgomery Clift: A Biography* (New York: Harcourt Brace Jovanovich, 1978), 295.

57 "gone on the wagon . . .": Interview with Kevin McCarthy, January 16, 2008. (All McCarthy quotations are from this interview.)

59 "Get those goddamned cameras . . .": Elizabeth Taylor, quoted by McCarthy.

60 "They are two of a kind": Heymann, *Liz*, 157.

60 Mike Todd and Fred Waller at the 1939 World's Fair: Avery Gilbert, *What the Nose Knows: The Science of Scent in Everyday Life* (New York: Crown, 2008), 154.

61 "The nose is really a sex organ . . .": Tony Kushner, *Angels in America, Part Two: Perestroika* (1995), act 1, scene 6.

62 Smell-O-Vision vs. AromaRama: Gilbert, *What the Nose Knows*, 154–63.

63 "At one point, the audience . . .": *Time*, quoted in ibid, 161.

64 "Tenn always joked . . .": James Grissom to M. G. Lord, e-mail, July 31, 2010.

64 "He advised strangers . . .": Meade Roberts, quoted in Heymann, 180.

65 "to her front": Carrie Fisher, *Wishful Drinking* (New York: Simon & Schuster, 2008), 34.

65 "America's Sweethearts": Ibid., 36.

66 "Mike's dead . . .": Hedda Hopper, quoted in Mann, *How to Be a Movie Star*, 228.

66 "kitchen date": Debbie Reynolds and Bob Thomas, *If I Knew Then* (New York: Bernard Geis Associates, 1962), 9.

66 "Saying Grace . . .": Ibid.,116.

67 SORRY TO DISAPPOINT . . .: Sam Spiegel, quoted in Natasha

Fraser-Cavassoni, *Sam Spiegel: The Incredible Life and Times of Hollywood's Most Iconoclastic Producer, the Miracle Worker Who Went from Penniless Refugee to Show Biz Legend, and Made Possible* The African Queen, On the Waterfront, The Bridge on the River Kwai, *and* Lawrence of Arabia (New York: Simon & Schuster, 2003), 209.

8. *Suddenly, Last Summer*, 1959

68 More women than men receiving lobotomies: Jack El-Hai, *The Lobotomist: A Maverick Medical Genius and His Tragic Quest to Rid the World of Mental Illness* (Hoboken, NJ: John Wiley & Sons, 2005), 290.

69 Maiming of Rosemary Kennedy: Ibid., 173–74.

69 Freeman nominated Moniz for Nobel Prize: El-Hai, *The Lobotomist*, 226–27.

70 "lobotomobile": Randy Kennedy, "A Filmmaker Inspired by Lobotomy," *New York Times*, April 29, 2004, http://www.nytimes.com/2004/04/29/movies/a-filmmaker-inspired-by-lobotomy.html?scp=1&sq=lobotomobile&st=cse.

70 American Academy of Pediatrics: Pam Belluck, "Group Backs Ritual 'Nick' as Female Circumcision Option," *New York Times*, May 6, 2010, http://www.nytimes.com/2010/05/07/health/policy/07cuts.html?scp=1&sq=u.s.%20doctors%20clitorectomy%202010&st=cse.

75 "They have so many of these torture groups . . .": Interview with Gore Vidal, Los Angeles, March 19, 2008. (All Vidal quotations are from this interview.)

75 "Galileans": Gore Vidal, *Julian* (New York: Signet Classics, 1964), 21.

77 "Ingmar Mankiewicz": Sam Spiegel, quoted by Vidal.

77 "The story admittedly deals with . . .": Quoted in Geoffrey M. Shurlock, memo, May 25, 1959, *Suddenly, Last Summer* Production Code Archive, Margaret Herrick Library, AMPAS.

77 "I don't need to tell you . . ." Geoffrey M. Shurlock to Sam Spiegel, letter, November 16, 1959, in ibid.

77 "the most bizarre film . . .": *Variety*, quoted in Mann, *How to Be a Movie Star*, 272.

78 "Cathy knew she was being used for evil.": Ad for *Suddenly, Last Summer,* quoted in Kelley, *Elizabeth Taylor*, 143.

9. *BUtterfield 8*, 1960

79 "There should be developed . . .": E. G. Dougherty, Production Code Administration memo, October 16, 1959, *BUtterfield 8* Production Code Archive, Margaret Herrick Library, AMPAS. (All Production Code Administration correspondence and memos are from this archive.)

80 "nymphomaniac": Geoffrey M. Shurlock to Robert Vogel, letter, October 12, 1959.

80 "sex where our agency is denied": Rebecca Walker, "Lusting for Freedom," in *Listen Up: Voices from the Next Feminist Generation*, ed. Barbara Findlen (Emeryville, CA: Seal Press, 2001), 23.

80 "For giving bodies . . .": Ibid.

80 "Confronted with a right-wing backlash . . .": Ellen Willis, *No More Nice Girls: Countercultural Essays* (Hanover: Wesleyan University Press, 1992), 20.

83 "norm of white procreative heterosexuality": Eva Pendleton, "Love for Sale: Queering Heterosexuality," in *Whores and Other Feminists*, ed. Jill Nagle (New York: Routledge, 1997), 73.

83 "Heterosexuality as a social system . . .": Ibid.

84 "separate themselves from the lower orders": Laura Kipnis, *Bound and Gagged: Pornography and the Politics of Fantasy in America* (New York: Grove Press, 1996), 173.

85 Gloria must be portrayed as "sick": Dougherty, Production Code Administration memo, October 16, 1959.

86 "rewritten so as to eliminate . . .": Dougherty, Production Code Administration memo, August 14, 1959.

86 "Liggett appears to have no recognition . . .": Geoffrey M. Shurlock to Robert Vogel, letter, October 27, 1959.

86 "From that moment on . . .": John O'Hara, *BUtterfield 8* (New York: Modern Library, 2003), 33.

86 "MGM must have thought . . .": Eddie Fisher, *My Life, My Loves* (New York: Harper & Row, 1981), 167.

87 "The trouble had nothing to do with the fact that Gloria was a call girl . . .": Pandro S. Berman, quoted in Maddox, *Who's Afraid of Elizabeth Taylor?* 154.

87 "trash": Fisher, *My Life, My Loves*, 168.

87 "a non-actor . . .": *Saturday Review*, "Butterfield 8," November 19, 1960.

88 Fisher details the "No Sale" incident in *My Life, My Loves*, 168–69.

88 "moral story": Geoffrey M. Shurlock to Eric Johnston, letter, May 25, 1961.

88 "sentimentally": Ibid.

88 "exactly the way it should . . .": Ibid.

88 "In the last century . . .": Ibid.

89 "I love prostitution . . .": Gustave Flaubert, quoted in Charles Bernheimer, *Figures of Ill Repute: Representing Prostitution in Nineteenth-century France* (Durham, NC: Duke University Press, 1997), 134.

89 "The ending is absurd": Bosley Crowther, "Elizabeth Taylor at 'Butterfield 8,'" *New York Times*, November 17, 1960.

10. 1960–1962

90 Taylor's injuries in childhood: Heymann, *Liz*, 39.

90 Fisher discusses Taylor's 1957 surgery in Fisher, *My Life, My Loves*, 128.

90 Todd's purchases are detailed in Kelley, *Elizabeth Taylor*, 108.

91 Fisher discusses emergency rooms in Fisher, *My Life, My Loves*.

92 "Get me my lip gloss": Ibid., 167.

92 Fisher details the Philadelphia accident in ibid., 170.

92 Taylor offends the British Hairdressers' Union: Amburn, *The Most Beautiful Woman in the World*, 124.

93 Fisher details the tracheotomy in Fisher, *My Life, My Loves*, 183–84.

94 "Hundreds of people . . .": Ibid, 184.

94 SIX THOUSAND . . . : Walter Wanger, *My Life with Cleopatra* (London: Corgi Books, 1963), 67.

94 "Dying, as I remember it . . .": Elizabeth Taylor, quoted in Kelley, *Elizabeth Taylor,* 165.

95 "I lost to a tracheotomy": Shirley MacLaine, quoted in Amburn, *The Most Beautiful Woman in the World,* 129.

95 "MGM's Little Miss Mammary": Richard Burton, quoted in Kelley, *Elizabeth Taylor,* 177

95 "elegant in a simple yellow silk gown": Wanger, *My Life with Cleopatra,* 120.

95 "handsome, arrogant, and vigorous": Ibid.

95 "you could almost feel the electricity": Ibid.

95 "erotic vagrancy": *L'Osservatore della Domenica,* quoted in Kelley, *Elizabeth Taylor,* 184.

11. *Cleopatra,* 1963

97 "Alexandria had its share . . .": Stacy Schiff, *Cleopatra: A Life* (New York: Little, Brown, 2010), 35.

98 Monroe fired from *Something's Got to Give*: Detailed by Maddox, *Who's Afraid of Elizabeth Taylor?* 171.

98 "I have a healthy aunt in Vienna . . .": Billy Wilder, quoted in Wanger, *My Life with Cleopatra,* 5.

99 Mankiewicz begged Zanuck: Joseph Mankiewicz to Darryl Zanuck. October 22, 1962, "Correspondence and Clippings on Cleopatra" collection, Margaret Herrick Library, AMPAS.

100 "women than ever before . . .": Betty Friedan, *The Feminine Mystique* (New York: Dell, 1983), 311.

101 "the forfeited self": Ibid., 310.

101 "How soon, how soon . . .": Carlo Maria Franzero, *The Life and Times of Cleopatra* (London: Heron Books, 1968), 10.

102 "that touch of frailty . . .": Ibid., 11.

104 "army of 4,000 . . .": "Liz is Back as Enchantress of Egypt," *Life*, October 6, 1961, 100.

104 "for naval engagements": Ibid.

104 "Cool-Chassis": Ibid., 112A.

104 "Automatic Picture Contrast Resolution": Ibid., 18.

104 "Golden Tube Sentry Unit": Ibid., 126–28.

104 Mankiewicz's use of amphetamines: Kelley, *Elizabeth Taylor*, 170.

106 "Miss Taylor is monotony . . .": *New Statesman*, cited in ibid., 191.

106 Martinez's work is detailed in Chip Brown, "The Search for Cleopatra," *National Geographic*, July 2011, 40–63.

107 Number of ballets, operas, plays, and films about Cleopatra are detailed in ibid., 45.

108 "I am fire and air": William Shakespeare, *Antony and Cleopatra*, act 5, scene 2.

108 "infinite variety": Ibid., act 2, scene 2.

12. 1963–1965

110 "This is a man who sold out": Richard Burton's agent, quoted in "The Man on the Billboard," *Time*, April 26, 1963, 70.

110 "Richard professionally is . . .": Paul Scofield, quoted in ibid.

110 "she was spread-eagled . . .": "Elizabeth Taylor Speaks Out," *Life*, December 18, 1964, 78.

111 The Burtons' meeting with Trumbo in London: Dalton Trumbo to Martin Ransohoff, letter (possibly unsent), February 18, 1965, Dalton Trumbo Archive, Charles E. Young Research Library, UCLA.

13. *The Sandpiper*, 1965

112 "As regards the individual nature . . .": Thomas Aquinas, *Summa Theologica*, question 91, article 1, reply objection 1.

112 "Any woman . . .": Gloria Steinem, "Sisterhood," *New York Magazine*, December 20, 1971, 46.

115 "been dull and devoid of ideas . . .": Dalton Trumbo to Martin Ransohoff, letter (possibly unsent), February 18, 1965, Dalton Trumbo Archive, Charles E. Young Research Library, UCLA.

115 The Burtons' meeting with Trumbo in London: Ibid.

115 "a lady's magazine melodrama": Richard Burton, quoted in Dalton Trumbo to Martin Ransohoff, letter, February 18, 1965, in ibid.

116 "There came a time . . .": Dalton Trumbo to Martin Ransohoff, letter accompanying changes to the script, August 10, 1964, in ibid.

116 "Beauty needs more tact . . .": Edith Wharton, *Novels* (New York: Library of America, 1985), 36.

118 "uses the formidable Miss Taylor . . .": Bosley Crowther, "Love Along Big Sur Seacoast," *New York Times*, July 16, 1965.

119 "Taylor demurely . . .": Pauline Kael, *Kiss Kiss Bang Bang* (New York: Bantam Books, 1969), 432.

119 The Production Code's position on nudity in *The Sandpiper* is detailed in a letter from Geoffrey M. Shurlock to Robert Vogel, July 9, 1964. (The full quote: "At no time should there be any exposure of her breasts.") AMPAS Production Code Archive, Margaret Herrick Library, AMPAS.

120 "empathy with the plight of one's companions . . .": Leonard Shlain, *The Alphabet Versus the Goddess: The Conflict Between Word and Image* (New York: Viking, 1998), 338.

120 "work, goals, focus . . .": Ibid.

120 "cruelty, argument, a disregard for nature . . .": Ibid.

14. *Who's Afraid of Virginia Woolf?* 1966

122 "The adjusted and cured . . .": Friedan, *The Feminine Mystique*, 311.

122 "The famous problem . . .": Richard Schickel, "What Film Has Done for Virginia," *Life*, July 22, 1966, 8.

122 Nichols and Lehman's tough decision is detailed in Thomas Thompson, "Raw Dialogue Challenges All the Censors," *Life*, June 10, 1966, 92.

123 "daughters of educated men": Woolf, *Three Guineas*, 18.

125 Edith Oliver, "The Current Cinema," *New Yorker*, July 2, 1966, 65.

126 from "comic stridency" to "the desperation . . ."; "fully deserves . . .": Schickel, "What Film Has Done for Virginia," 8.

126 "an aging maneater" who has "a father fixation . . .": *Time*, "Marital Armageddon," July 1, 1966.

126 "has not really written about men . . .": *Newsweek*, "Who's Afraid . . . ," July 4, 1966.

127 "I think it's a marvelous film": Geoffrey M. Shurlock, quoted in Thompson, "Raw Dialogue Challenges All the Censors," 96.

127 *Kiss Me, Stupid*: Shurlock's embarrassment is detailed in ibid.

127 *goddam*, *screw you*, etc.: Geoffrey M. Shurlock to Jack Warner, letter, March 26, 1963, *Who's Afraid of Virginia Woolf?* Production Code Archive, Margaret Herrick Library, AMPAS.

127 Appeal to review board: Thompson, "Raw Dialogue Challenges All the Censors," 98.

128 "The only possible favorable comment . . .": Catholic volunteer, quoted in ibid., 96.

128 "Disguising profanity . . .": Mike Nichols, quoted in ibid., 92.

15. 1967–1973

130 "bonny Kate" and "Kate the curst": William Shakespeare, *Taming of the Shrew*, act 2, scene 1.

131 "skirt every pan": Interview with Richard McWhorter, Los Angeles, August 21, 2010. (All McWhorter quotations are from this interview.)

131 "serve, love and obey": Shakespeare, *Taming of the Shrew*, act 5, scene 2.

131 "I am ashamed . . .": Ibid.

132 "You have made my original book . . .": Carson McCullers to John Huston, Chapman Mortimer, and Gladys Hill, letter,

October 11, 1966, John Huston Archive, Margaret Herrick Library, AMPAS.

133 "What other movie queen . . .": Gloria Steinem to Ray Stark, undated memo, in ibid.

133 "More guys than you can imagine . . .": Interview with Robert Forster, Los Angeles, April 10, 2008. (All Forster quotations are from this interview.)

134 "Hell hath no fury . . .": Bosley Crowther, "Sex, Shock and Sensibility," *New York Times*, October 22, 1967, http://select.nytimes.com/gst/abstract.html?res=F5071FFA3A55107A93C0AB178BD95F438685F9&scp=4&sq=Crowther%20review%20Reflections%20Golden%20Eye&st=cse.

136 "holds all the joy of standing at an autopsy": *Variety*, quoted in Amburn, *The Most Beautiful Woman in the World*, 219.

16. *Ash Wednesday*, 1973

139 "a fucking lousy nothing . . .": Richard Burton to photographer Gianni Bozzachi, letter, April 27, 1973. Photograph of handwritten letter and transcription in RR Auction catalog for a sale on June 15, 2011. http://www.icollector.com/Richard-Burton_i10646841.

139 "Lumpy and "Pockface": Kelley, *Elizabeth Taylor*, 258.

140 "I'm sure Taylor did support the Equal Rights Amendment . . .": Liz Smith to M. G. Lord, e-mail, March 31, 2009.

141 "a hoot": Interview with Kate Burton, New York City,

May 14, 2010. (All Kate Burton quotations are from this interview.)

141 "Eating became one . . .": Taylor, *Elizabeth Takes Off*, 44.

142 "John went his way . . .": Ibid., 45.

142 "the wife of some dim dilettante . . .": Garry Trudeau, *A Tad Overweight, but Violet Eyes to Die For* (New York: Holt, Rinehart, and Winston, 1979), 8.

142 "domestic Siberia": Taylor, *Elizabeth Takes Off*, 42.

142 Meeting with Zev Buffman: Mann, *How to Be a Movie Star*, 404.

17. *The Little Foxes*, 1981

143 "I'm going to be alive . . .": Lillian Hellman, *Six Plays by Lillian Hellman* (New York: Vintage Books, 179), 198.

143 "What if this woman . . .": Interview with Austin Pendleton, New York City, August 13, 2008. (All Pendleton quotations are from this interview.)

146 "Miss Taylor is no cardboard harridan . . .": Frank Rich, "Stage: The Missus Taylor and Stapleton in 'Foxes,'" *New York Times*, May 8, 1981, http://www.nytimes.com/1981/05/08/theater/stage-the-misses-taylor-and-stapleton-in-foxes.html?scp=5&sq=rich%20little%20foxes%20review&st=cse.

146 "I'm really Alexandra . . .": Conversation between Lillian Hellman and Elizabeth Taylor as recalled by Pendleton.

18. 1982–1984

149 "Richard Burton looked at me . . .": Pendleton interview.

149 "I have to talk to you . . .": Ibid.

150 "He had an eye": McWhorter interview.

150 "I never touched a drop . . .": Taylor, *Elizabeth Takes Off*, 98.

151 "all the vitality . . ." Frank Rich, "Theater: 'Private Lives' Burton and Miss Taylor," *New York Times*, May 9, 1983, http://www.nytimes.com/1983/05/09/theater/theater-private-lives-burton-and-miss-taylor.html?scp=2&sq=%22private%20lives%22%20frank%20rich&st=cse.

151 "family intervention": Taylor, *Elizabeth Takes Off*, 99.

151 "The entire process . . .": Ibid., 100.

153 Taylor cooled to Colacello: Conversation with Bob Colacello, Los Angeles, November 9, 2008.

153 "Debauched Mary": Bob Colacello, *Holy Terror: Andy Warhol Close Up* (New York: HarperCollins, 1990), 154.

153 The leaf plucking is detailed in ibid., 156–57.

153 "big fat joints of Brazilian marijuana . . .": Ibid., 346.

153 "No movie . . .": Liz Smith to M. G. Lord, e-mail, March 31, 2009.

154 "Its three roots . . .": Taylor, *Elizabeth Takes Off*, 105.

154 "She has been surrounded . . .": Smith to Lord, e-mail, March 31, 2009.

155 "It was her greatest conscious gift": Burton interview.

19. Her Greatest Conscious Gift, 1984–2011

157 "A woman who advertised . . .": Woolf, *Three Guineas*, 30.

157 " "the judgment of God . . .": Falwell's *Old Time Gospel Hour*, August 7, 1983.

158 "We were young doctors . . .": Interview with Michael Gottlieb, Los Angeles, May 18, 2011. (All Gottlieb quotations are from this interview.)

159 "Why did they bring him . . .": Interview with Francine Hanberg, Los Angeles, October 6, 2010.

162 "lame-dog causes . . .": Frank Sinatra, quoted in Taraborelli, *Elizabeth*, 397.

162 "When I saw that my fame . . .": Elizabeth Taylor, quoted in Liz Smith, "Elizabeth Taylor, Close Up," *Architectural Digest*, July 2011, 64.

162 "At a time when disgust . . .": Sean Strub's remembrance in Kevin Sessums, Elizabeth Taylor Interview About Her AIDS Advocacy, *Daily Beast*, March 23, 2011, http://www.thedailybeast.com/articles/2011/03/23/elizabeth-taylor-interview-about-her-aids-advocacy-plus-stars-remember.html.

164 "On a personal level . . .": Telephone interview with Dr. David Ho, November 18, 2010.

164 "love of the work itself": Woolf, *Three Guineas*, 171.

164 "wildly exaggerated": Interview with Sally Morrison, Los Angeles, October 20, 2011.

165 "Working at the age of nine . . .": Elizabeth Taylor, interview by Larry King, May 30, 2006.

165 "I really was concerned . . .": Burton interview.

165 "I don't see her . . .": Ibid.

166 "No RIP Elizabeth Taylor . . .": Margie Phelps, quoted in *Huffington Post*, "Westboro Baptist Church to Picket Elizabeth Taylor Funeral: March 24, 2011, http://www.huffingtonpost.com/2011/03/24/westboro=baptist=church=elizabeth=taylor_n_839979.html.

166 "Feminism is . . .": Pollitt in "Rebecca Traister, Hanna Rosin, and Others."

166 "her greatest conscious gift": Burton interview.

167 "all of us who were HIV positive . . .": Sessums, Elizabeth Taylor Interview.

Bibliography

Alpert, Hollis. "A Double Bounty from Hollywood." *Saturday Review of Literature*, September 1, 1951, 28–31.

Amburn, Ellis. *The Most Beautiful Woman in the World: The Obsessions, Passions and Courage of Elizabeth Taylor.* New York: HarperCollins, 2000.

Appignanesi, Lisa. *Mad, Bad and Sad: Women and the Mind Doctors.* New York: W. W. Norton, 2008.

Bagnold, Enid. *National Velvet.* New York: HarperFestival, 2002.

Basinger, Jeanine. *The Star Machine.* New York: Alfred A. Knopf, 2007.

———. *A Woman's View: How Hollywood Spoke to Women, 1930–1960.* Hanover, NH: Wesleyan University Press, 1993.

Baxter, Charles. *The Art of Subtext: Beyond Plot.* St. Paul, MN: Graywolf Press, 2007.

Bayer, Ronald. *AIDS Doctors: Voices from the Epidemic: An Oral History.* New York: Oxford University Press, 2002.

Belluck, Pam. "Group Backs Ritual 'Nick' as Female Circumcision Option." *New York Times,* May 6, 2010, http://www.nytimes.com/2010/05/07/health/policy/07cuts.html?scp=1&sq=u.s.%20doctors%20clitorectomy%202010&st=cse.

Bernheimer, Charles. *Figures of Ill Repute: Representing Prostitution in Nineteenth-century France.* Durham, NC: Duke University Press, 1997.

Bernstein, Matthew. *Walter Wanger: Hollywood Independent.* Minneapolis: University of Minnesota Press, 2000.

Biskind, Peter. *Easy Riders, Raging Bulls: How the Sex-Drugs-and-Rock 'n' Roll Generation Saved Hollywood.* New York: Simon & Schuster, 1998.

———. *Seeing Is Believing: How Hollywood Taught Us to Stop Worrying and Love the Fifties.* New York: Pantheon Books, 1983.

Black, Gregory. *The Catholic Crusade Against the Movies, 1940–1975.* Cambridge: Cambridge University Press, 1998.

Bogdanovich, Peter, ed. *The Best American Movie Writing.* New York: St. Martin's Griffin, 1999.

Bosworth, Patricia. *Montgomery Clift: A Biography.* New York: Harcourt Brace Jovanovich, 1978.

Braudy, Leo. *The Frenzy of Renown: Fame and Its History.* New York; Vintage Books, 1997.

Breines, Wini. *Young, White and Miserable: Growing Up Female in the Fifties.* Boston: Beacon Press, 1992.

Brown, Chip. "The Search for Cleopatra." *National Geographic,* July 2011, 40–63.

Brown, Frederick. *Flaubert: A Biography.* Cambridge, MA: Harvard University Press, 2007.

Brownmiller, Susan. *Femininity.* New York: Ballantine Books, 1985.

Chesler, Phyllis. *Women and Madness: When is a Woman Mad and Who is It Who Decides?* New York: Doubleday, 1972.

"Cinema: The New Pictures." *Time,* September 10, 1951, http://www.time.com/time/magazine/article/0,9171,815385,00.html.

Colacello, Bob. *Holy Terror: Andy Warhol Close Up*. New York: HarperCollins, 1990.

Cook, Bruce. *Dalton Trumbo*. New York: Charles Scribner's Sons, 1977.

Crowther, Bosley. "Elizabeth Taylor at Butterfield 8." *New York Times*, November 17, 1960.

———. "Love Along Big Sur Seacoast." *New York Times*, July 16, 1965.

Dick, Bernard F. *Anatomy of Film*. New York: St. Martin's Press, 1998.

Doherty, Thomas. *Hollywood's Censor: Joseph I. Breen and the Production Code Administration*. New York: Columbia University Press, 2007.

Dreiser, Theodore. *An American Tragedy*. New York: Library of America, 2003.

El-hai, Jack. *The Lobotomist: A Maverick Medical Genius and His Tragic Quest to Rid the World of Mental Illness*. Hoboken, NJ: John Wiley & Sons, 2005.

"Elizabeth Taylor Speaks Out." *Life*, December 18, 1964, 74–85.

Evans, Sara. *Personal Politics: The Roots of the Women's Liberation in the Civil Rights Movement and the New Left*. New York: Vintage Books, 1980.

Faludi, Susan. *Backlash: The Undeclared War Against American Women*. New York: Crown, 1991.

Ferber, Edna. *Giant*. New York: Perennial Classics, 1980.

Findlen, Barbara, ed. *Listen Up: Voices from the Next Feminist Generation*. Emeryville, CA: Seal Press, 2001.

Fisher, Carrie. *Wishful Drinking*. New York: Simon & Schuster, 2008.

Fisher, Eddie. *My Life, My Loves*. New York: Harper & Row, 1981.

Franzero, Carlo Maria. *The Life and Times of Cleopatra.* London: Heron Books, 1968.

Fraser-Cavassoni, Natasha. *Sam Spiegel: The Incredible Life and Times of Hollywood's Most Iconoclastic Producer, the Miracle Worker Who Went from Penniless Refugee to Show Biz Legend, and Made Possible* The African Queen, On the Waterfront, The Bridge on the River Kwai, *and* Lawrence of Arabia. New York: Simon & Schuster, 2003.

Friedan, Betty. *The Feminine Mystique.* New York: Dell, 1983.

Gabler, Neal. *An Empire of Their Own: How the Jews Invented Hollywood.* New York: Anchor Books, 1989.

Gilbert, Avery. *What the Nose Knows: The Science of Scent in Everyday Life.* New York: Crown, 2008.

Goldfarb, Brad. "Talking to Elton John." *Interview,* February 2007, 207.

Goleman, Daniel. *Emotional Intelligence: Why It Can Matter More Than IQ.* New York: Bantam Books, 1996.

Greenberg, Clement. "Art." *The Nation,* April 7, 1945, 397–98

Harris, Mark. *Pictures at a Revolution.* New York: Penguin Books, 2008.

Haskell, Molly. *Frankly, My Dear: Gone With the Wind Revisited.* New Haven & London: Yale University Press, 2009.

———. *From Reverence to Rape*: *The Treatment of Women in the Movies.* Chicago and London: University of Chicago Press, 1987.

Hellman, Lillian. *Six Plays by Lillian Hellman.* New York: Vintage Books, 1979.

Heymann, C. David. *Liz: An Intimate Biography of Elizabeth Taylor.* New York: Birch Lane, 1995.

Heywood, Leslie, and Jennifer Drake, eds. *Third Wave Agenda: Be-*

ing Feminist, Doing Feminism. Minneapolis: University of Minnesota Press, 1997.

"History of Cinema Series: Hollywood and the Production Code." Department of Special Collections, Margaret Herrick Library, Academy of Motion Picture Arts and Sciences.

hooks, bell. *Feminism is for Everybody: Passionate Politics.* London: Pluto Press, 2000.

Hopper, Hedda. "When a Girl Marries." *Modern Screen*, November 1956, 56–57, 95–97.

Huston, John. Archive. Margaret Herrick Library, Academy of Motion Picture Arts and Sciences.

Jervis, Lisa, and Andi Zeisler. *Bitchfest: Ten Years of Cultural Criticism from the Pages of* Bitch *Magazine.* New York: Farrar, Straus & Giroux, 2006.

Kael, Pauline. *Kiss Kiss Bang Bang.* New York: Bantam Books, 1969.

Kelley, Kitty. *Elizabeth Taylor: The Last Star.* New York: Simon & Schuster, 2001.

Kennedy, Randy. "A Filmmaker Inspired by Lobotomy." *New York Times*, April 29, 2004, http://www.nytimes.com/2004/04/29/movies/a-filmmaker-inspired-by-lobotomy.html?scp=1&sq=lobotomobile&st=cse.

Kipnis, Laura. *Bound and Gagged: Pornography and the Politics of Fantasy in America.* New York: Grove Press, 1996.

Kramarae, Cheris, and Paula A. Treichler. *A Feminist Dictionary.* Boston: Pandora Press, 1985.

Kushner, Tony. *Angels in America, Part Two: Perestroika* (1995). New York: Theatre Communication Group, 2009.

Labaton, Vivien, and Dawn Lundy Martin. *The Fire This Time: Young Activists and the New Feminism.* New York: Anchor Books, 2004.

Levine, Barry. "A Career in Tabloids, Thanks to Elizabeth Taylor." *New York Times*, March 26, 2011, http://www.nytimes.com/2011/03/27/opinion/27levine.html.

"Liz is Back as Enchantress of Egypt," *Life*, October 6, 1961, 93–100.

Lower, Cheryl Bray, and R. Barton Palmer, eds. *Joseph L. Mankiewicz: Critical Essays with an Annotated Bibliography and a Filmography.* Jefferson, NC: McFarland, 2001.

McGrath, Charles. "The Study of Men (or Males)." *New York Times*, January 7, 2011, http://www.nytimes.com/2011/01/09/education/09men-t.html.

McLellan, Diana. *The Girls: Sappho Goes to Hollywood.* New York: St. Martin's Press, 2000.

Maddox, Brenda. *Who's Afraid of Elizabeth Taylor?* New York: M. Evans, 1977.

"The Man on the Billboard." *Time*, April 26, 1963, 70–74.

Mann, William J. *How to Be a Movie Star: Elizabeth Taylor in Hollywood.* Boston: Houghton Mifflin Harcourt, 2009.

———. *Kate: The Woman Who Was Hepburn.* New York: Henry Holt, 2006.

Nagle, Jill, ed. *Whores and Other Feminists.* New York: Routledge, 1997.

O'Hara, John. *BUtterfield 8.* New York: Modern Library, 2003.

Oliver, Edith. "The Current Cinema," *New Yorker*, July 2, 1966, 65.

Orbach, Susie. *Fat Is a Feminist Issue.* New York: Berkeley Publishing Group, 1979.

Paglia, Camille. "Elizabeth Taylor: Hollywood's Pagan Queen." *Penthouse*, March 1992. Reprinted in *Sex, Art, and American Culture.* New York: Vintage Books, 1992.

Percy, Walker. *The Moviegoer.* New York: Ballantine Books, 1990.

Phillips, Bianca. "The Dalai Lama Is a Feminist/The Daily Buzz." *Memphis Flyer,* September 23, 2009, http://www.memphisflyer.com/TheDailyBuzz/archives/2009/09/23/the-dalai-lama-is-a-feminist.

Pollitt, Katha. *Reasonable Creatures: Essays on Women and Feminism.* New York: Alfred A. Knopf, 1994.

"Rebecca Traister, Hanna Rosin, and Others on Why You Can't Own Feminism." *Slate*, October 8, 2010, http://www.slate.com/id/2270053/entry/2270054.

Reynolds, Debbie, and Bob Thomas. *If I Knew Then.* New York: Bernard Geis Associates, 1962.

Rich, Frank, "Theater: 'Private Lives' Burton and Miss Taylor," *New York Times*, May 9, 1983.

Riva, Maria. *Marlene Dietrich.* New York: Ballantine Books, 1994.

Roiphe, Katie. *East Night in Paradise*: *Sex and Morals at the Century's End*. Boston: Little, Brown, 1997.

Rosin, Hannah. "The End of Men." *The Atlantic,* July/August 2010, http://www.theatlantic.com/magazine/archive/2010/05/the-end-of-men/8135/.

Royster, Francesca T. *Becoming Cleopatra: The Shifting Image of an Icon.* New York: Palgrave Macmillan, 2003.

Schickel, Richard. "What Film Has Done for Virginia." *Life,* July 22, 1966, 8.

Schiff, Stacy. *Cleopatra: A Life.* New York: Little, Brown, 2010.

Sessums, Kevin. Elizabeth Taylor Interview About Her AIDS Advocacy. *Daily Beast*, March 23, 2011, http://www.thedailybeast.com/articles/2011/03/23/elizabeth-taylor-interview-about-her-aids-advocacy-plus-stars-remember.html.

Shear, Marie. "Media Watch: Celebrating Women's Words." *New Directions for Women*, May/June 1986, 6.

Shlain, Leonard. *The Alphabet Versus the Goddess: The Conflict Between Word and Image*. New York: Viking, 1998.

Siegel, Deborah. *Sisterhood, Interrupted: From Radical Women to Girls Gone Wild*. New York: Palgrave Macmillan, 2007.

Siegel, Larry, and Mort Drucker. "The Sinpiper." In *The Worst from MAD*, 75–79. New York: E. C. Publications, 1968.

Smith, Liz. "Elizabeth Taylor, Close Up." *Architectural Digest*, July 2011, 64.

———. "Liz Taylor Returning to Stage," *New York Post*, August 23, 2007.

Steinem, Gloria. *Marilyn*. New York: Plume, 1987.

———. "Sisterhood." *New York Magazine*, December 20, 1971, 46.

Stevens, George. Archive. Margaret Herrick Library, Academy of Motion Picture Arts and Sciences.

Story, Louise. "Many Women at Elite Colleges Set Career Path to Motherhood." *New York Times*, September 20, 2005, http://www.nytimes.com/2005/09/20/national/20women.html.

Taraborelli, Randy. *Elizabeth*. New York: Warner Books, 2006.

Taylor, Elizabeth. *Elizabeth Takes Off: On Weight Gain, Weight Loss, Self-Image, and Self-Esteem*. New York: Putnam, 1987.

———. *Nibbles and Me*. New York: Simon & Schuster Children's Publishing, 2002.

Thompson, Thomas. "Raw Dialogue Challenges All the Censors." *Life*, June 10, 1966, 92, 96–98.

Thomson, David. *America in the Dark: Hollywood and the Gift of Unreality*. New York: William Morrow, 1997.

Trudeau, Garry. *A Tad Overweight, but Violet Eyes to Die For.* New York: Holt, Rinehart, and Winston, 1979.

Trumbo, Dalton. Archive. Charles E. Young Research Library, University of California, Los Angeles.

Valenti, Jessica. *Full Frontal Feminism: A Young Woman's Guide to Why Feminism Matters.* Berkeley, CA: Seal Press, 2007.

Vidal, Gore. Archive. Houghton Library, Harvard College Library, Harvard University.

———. *Julian.* New York: Signet Classics, 1964.

———. *United States: Essays, 1952–1992.* New York: Broadway Books, 1993.

Walker, Alexander. *Elizabeth: The Life of Elizabeth Taylor.* New York: Grove Press, 2001.

Walker, Barbara G. *The Skeptical Feminist: Discovering the Virgin, Mother, and Crone.* San Francisco: Harper & Row, 1987.

Walker, Rebecca. "Becoming the Third Wave." *Ms.*, January/February 1992, 39–41.

———. "Lusting for Freedom." In *Listen Up: Voices of the Next Feminist Generation*, ed. Barbara Findlen, 19–24. Emeryville, CA: Seal Press, 2001.

———, ed. *To Be Real: Telling the Truth and Changing the Face of Feminism.* New York: Anchor Books, 1995.

Wanger, Walter, and Joe Hyams. *My Life with Cleopatra.* London: Corgi Books, 1963.

West, Rebecca. "Mr. Chesterton in Hysterics." Reprinted in *The Young Rebecca: The Writings of Rebecca West, 1911–17*, ed. Jane Marcus. New York: Virago Press, 1982.

Wharton, Edith. *Novels.* New York: Library of America, 1985.

Williams, Tennessee. *Suddenly Last Summer.* New York: Dramatists Play Service, 1986.

Willis, Ellen. *No More Nice Girls: Countercultural Essays.* Hanover: Wesleyan University Press, 1992.

Wilson, Michael. Archive. Charles E. Young Research Library, University of California, Los Angeles.

Woolf, Virginia. *Three Guineas.* New York: Harcourt, Brace and Company, 1938.

Yardley, Jonathan. "Ferber's 'Giant' Cut Down to Size." *Washington Post,* May 8, 2006, http://www.washingtonpost.com/wp-dyn/content/article/2006/05/07/AR2006050701112.html.

Zeffirelli, Franco. *Zeffirelli: An Autobiography.* New York: Weidenfeld & Nicolson, 1986.

Index

Note: Most characters are indexed alphabetically by first name. Exceptions are those who are also historical figures, or for whom a first name is not available.

INDEX

INDEX

A Note on the Author

M. G. Lord is an acclaimed cultural critic and investigative journalist, and the author of the widely praised books *Forever Barbie: The Unauthorized Biography of a Real Doll* and *Astro Turf: The Private Life of Rocket Science*. Since 1995 she has been a frequent contributor to the *New York Times Book Review* and the *Times*'s Arts & Leisure section. Her work has appeared in numerous publications, including the *New Yorker*, *Vogue*, the *Wall Street Journal*, the *Los Angeles Times*, *Travel + Leisure*, the *Hollywood Reporter*, and *Artforum*. Before becoming a freelance writer, Lord was a syndicated political cartoonist and a columnist for *Newsday*. She teaches at the University of Southern California and lives in Los Angeles.